# The Art of
# Kyuki-Do®
# Martial Arts

Grand Master Ken Ok Hyung Kim

**3RD EDITION**
**Revised December 5, 2019**

**Written by Ken Ok Hyung Kim and Ken Blumreich.**
**Edited by Jeffrey Kim and Lloyd Holden.**
**Proofed by Daniel Williams.**
**Photography of forms by Annaliese Ashley.**
**Artwork and design by Carmen Champagne.**

# Preface and Welcome by Grand Master Ken Ok Hyung Kim

Dear Student,

On behalf of the American Kyuki-Do Federation and its members, I would like to welcome you.

Our Federation was established in 1979 with the help of several talented, devoted and sincere martial artists. You have now joined those individuals and will have the opportunity to share in the personal growth that is the hallmark of the true martial artist.

The American Kyuki-Do Federation is committed to helping our students grow spiritually, mentally and physically. It is my hope that your Kyuki-Do training will help you discover your own inner strength and develop and perfect both your mental health and your physical health.

This manual has been prepared for you so that you may become better acquainted with the philosophy and history of Kyuki-Do as well as its forms and techniques. This manual is intended to serve as a supplement for the quality instruction that you will receive in the dojang. I encourage you to read this manual thoroughly, as an understanding of the material presented in these pages will greatly assist you in your training.

Again, I warmly welcome you into our Federation and assure you that you will receive our full cooperation, encouragement and guidance in your quest for a sound mind, a healthy body and a strong spirit.

Sincerely,

Grand Master Ken Ok Hyung Kim
Founder of Kyuki-Do

Grand Master Ken Ok Hyung Kim
Founder of Kyuki-Do

# Table of Contents


Preface and Welcome by Grand Master Ken Ok Hyung Kim ....3
Table of Contents ....5
Chapter One: History and Background ....8
  Introduction: What Is Kyuki-Do? ....9
    Literal Translation of Kyuki-Do ....10
  Korean History ....11
    The Choson Period ....11
    The Three Kingdoms Period ....11
    The Shilla Dynasty ....12
    The Koryo Period ....12
    The Yi Dynasty ....12
    Modern Korea ....13
  History of the Martial Arts from Which Kyuki-Do Was Developed ....14
    History of Tae Kwon Do ....14
    History of Yudo/Judo ....14
    History of Brazilian Jiu Jitsu ....15
    History of Hapkido ....16
  History and Symbolism of the Flags ....17
    The American Flag ....17
    The Korean Flag ....19
    The American Kyuki-Do Federation Flag ....20
Chapter Two: Philosophy and Conduct ....21
  The Philosophy and Symbolism of Kyuki-Do ....22
    Purpose of Kyuki-Do ....23
    Eum and Yang ....23
    The Symbol of Kyuki-Do ....24
    Mind Body Spirit ....24
    Who I Am ....25
  Student Conduct ....26
    The Student Pledge ....26
    The Tenets of Kyuki-Do ....26
    General Rules for the Kyuki-Do Student ....27
    Dojang Rules and Etiquette ....27
Chapter Three: Training ....30
  Beginning Your Kyuki-Do Training ....31
    Developing Your Personal Workout Routine ....32
  The Bow (Kyung-nyeh) ....33
    Protocol for Bowing and Shaking Hands ....33
  Meditation ....34
  Kihap ....35
  Theory of Power ....36
  Strength ....38
  Total Physical Fitness ....39
Chapter Four: Application ....40

Breaking ........ 41
Physics of Breaking ........ 41
Target Areas ........ 42
One-Step Sparring ........ 45
Purpose of One-Step Sparring ........ 45
Types of One-Step Sparring ........ 45
Procedure for One-Step Sparring ........ 46
Sparring ........ 48
Sparring Rules ........ 48
Legal Aspects of Self-Defense ........ 50
Chapter Five: Weapons Training ........ 51
Kobudo History and Weapons ........ 52
Kobudo Weapons: Nunchaku ........ 53
Kobudo Weapons: Sai ........ 54
Kobudo Weapons: Kama ........ 54
Kobudo Weapons: Tonfa ........ 54
Filipino Kali Sticks ........ 56
Bo Staff ........ 57
Katana ........ 58
Weapons Form Criteria ........ 59
Chapter Six: Kyuki-Do and Its Forms ........ 60
The Meaning Behind the Forms ........ 61
The Belt Ranking System and the Meaning of the Belt Colors ........ 62
The Forms of Kyuki-Do ........ 64
Kibon ........ 65
Kicho ........ 70
Kyuki Il Chang ........ 78
Kyuki Yee Chang ........ 88
Kyuki Sam Chang ........ 97
Guen Bon ........ 107
Chon Ji In Il Chang ........ 117
Chon Ji In Yee Chang ........ 128
Chon Ji In Sam Chang ........ 140
Man Nam ........ 151
Ka Chi ........ 169
Sa Rang ........ 183
Kyuki-Do Nakbop Hyung ........ 195
Chapter Seven: Grand Master Ken Ok Hyung Kim ........ 208
Chapter Eight: Appendices ........ 211
Appendix A: Korean Terminology ........ 212
Terminology: Fighting Arts ........ 212
Terminology: General ........ 212
Terminology: Body Parts ........ 213
Terminology: Direction, Location and Movement ........ 213
Terminology: Class Commands ........ 214
Terminology: Counting ........ 214

Terminology: Greetings and Formalities ........ 215
Terminology: Categories of Techniques ........ 215
Terminology: Stances ........ 215
Terminology: Blocks ........ 216
Terminology: Strikes ........ 217
Terminology: Kicks ........ 218
Terminology: Falling ........ 219
Appendix B: Japanese Terminology ........ 220
Japanese Terminology: General ........ 220
Japanese Terminology: Tournaments and Class Commands ........ 220
Japanese Terminology: Categories of Techniques ........ 220
Japanese Terminology: Throws ........ 221
Japanese Terminology: Grappling Techniques ........ 223
Japanese Terminology: Falls ........ 224
Appendix C: Grand Master Kim's Personal Philosophy ........ 225
Elements, Energy and Environment ........ 225
Eum and Yang, and the Balance ........ 225
Divine Principle ........ 226
Appendix D: The Meaning and History of the AKF Black Belt Certificate ........ 227

# Chapter One: History and Background

The first portion of this handbook is intended to provide students of Kyuki-Do with the context and history of Kyuki-Do's development. An appreciation of the Korean culture and of the rich martial arts lineage that led to the creation of Kyuki-Do will help the student better understand the art.

# *Introduction: What Is Kyuki-Do?*

Kyuki-Do is a martial art that primarily incorporates elements of Tae Kwon Do, Hapkido and Judo. Kyuki-Do was introduced to the United States by Grand Master Ok Hyung Kim, the founder of the art. Grand Master Kim began teaching martial arts in the US in 1967 and went on to found the American Kyuki-Do Federation (Kyuki-Do's sanctioning body) in 1979.

Kyuki-Do is designed to be practical, versatile and effective at a variety of different ranges and in a variety of different situations. The Tae Kwon Do - derived kicks and strikes provide excellent power at medium and long range, while the throws, locks, chokes and joint manipulation of Judo and Hapkido allow for effective close-range fighting and grappling.

Kyuki-Do is a living, growing martial art that continues to expand and change. In addition to the core elements of Tae Kwon Do, Judo, Jiu Jitsu and Hapkido, Kyuki-Do also includes techniques from Karate, boxing, wrestling, traditional weapons from Okinawa and the Philippines, and many other arts and styles.

Kyuki-Do is more than just an effective system of self-defense; it is a martial art that encourages students to realize their own physical, mental and spiritual potential. Students of Kyuki-Do learn discipline, self-control, patience, persistence and respect for themselves and others. Students are expected to continually strive to perfect themselves, both in the dojang and in every other area of their life.

The term "art" as it is used in the context of Kyuki-Do means a method or technique used to demonstrate truth, perfection, elegance, perseverance and virtue. The art is a reality that we face in our daily life; the truth of the art is maintained in the midst of our society, and its virtue is seen in all of the most positive and beneficial attributes of humanity.

The art of Kyuki-Do should not be seen merely as a technique of fighting or a means of defeating an opponent. It should not be wielded as a destructive weapon used to demonstrate hatred, jealousy, pride, anger or arrogance. Those who use the art to pursue such motives are guilty of abuse and carelessness. Furthermore, they are ignorant of the underlying significance, principles and purpose of the art. It is important to remind such individuals of the tenets, purpose and philosophy of Kyuki-Do.

The knowledge taught by Kyuki-Do is unlimited; the more that we learn, the more we realize how little we actually know. The more our imperfection is revealed to us, the more we understand the deeper nature of the art. The student of Kyuki-Do must be devoted to the pursuit of the perfection of their own character. Perfection is, of course, a goal that can never be fully attained, but the students who devote themselves to endlessly striving towards this goal will find that they will continue to become better, stronger, healthier people. Progress in Kyuki-Do is measured by the student's physical and mental development, their humility, their self-control and their unwavering commitment to the goal of personal perfection.

Kyuki-Do requires the individual to develop a more responsible personality. It demands of the individual daily physical exercise and a constant search for new techniques and new applications of old techniques. It requires the perfection of these techniques and their application in a manner that is positive and beneficial to the student and to others.

If selfishness, hatred, dishonesty, anger, disrespect or bigotry still persist in an individual after a period of time spent studying Kyuki-Do, then that individual will need to start their training over again in order to find the real meaning of the martial arts.

## Literal Translation of Kyuki-Do

"Kyuk" means strike. "Ki" is energy. "Do" means art, path, way or method. "Kyuki-Do" then translates as "The way or the art of striking with energy."

In Korean, "Kyuki-Do" literally means "spark or explosion." The word signifies the sudden release or burst of energy that accompanies the successful execution of any fighting technique; it is a method of properly applying energy in order to strike an opponent or target with maximum force.

# *Korean History*

Korean history and pre-history can be divided into six stages: the Choson period, the Three Kingdoms period, the Shilla Dynasty, the Koryo period, the Yi Dynasty and Modern Korea.

## The Choson Period

Korea's origins date back to 2334 BC when, according to legend, the sky god Hwanin gave birth to Hwanung, who wished to descend from heaven and live in the world of human beings. Hwanung descended to Mount T'ae-baek and founded a great city. The legend goes on to explain that at this time a bear and a tiger living in the same cave prayed to Hwanung to transform them into human beings. Hwanung agreed to this; he gave them a bundle of sacred mugworts and twenty cloves of garlic and told them to eat the herbs and shun the daylight for 100 days. After 21 days, the bear became a woman, but the tiger was unable to follow Hwanung's command and therefore remained a beast.

In 2332 BC, the bear woman then prayed for a child, and after Hwanung lay with her she gave birth to Tangun Wanggum. Tangun founded the city of Pyongyang and called his country Choson. Tangun later moved his capital to Asadal on Mount Paegak.

Modern scholars theorize that this founding legend probably refers to the unification of several different tribes and clans during Korea's ancient history. The unification of these different tribes of people eventually resulted in the Kingdom of Ko-Choson (ancient Choson). Ko-Choson gradually attained more political and trade power and eventually rose as a center of ancient eastern culture.

Around the fourth century BC, Ko-Choson began to struggle with the Yan Kingdom of China across its borders. Eventually, during the first century BC, Ko-Choson's capital city was conquered by the forces of Han China, marking the end of Choson and the beginning of the Three Kingdoms period.

## The Three Kingdoms Period

The time from 57 BC to 668 AD was a contentious period in Korea's past marked by the emergence of three separate kingdoms. The Shilla Kingdom, founded in 57 BC, controlled the southern portion of Korea. The Koguryo Kingdom, founded in 37 BC, occupied the northern portion of the Korean peninsula, up to the Chinese border. The Paekche Kingdom, founded in 18 BC, also occupied parts of the south. It was during this time that Buddhism was first introduced to Korea.

The three kingdoms fought continuously with each other and with the Han Chinese. The Shilla eventually emerged victorious, defeating the Paekche in 660 AD and the Koguryo in 668 AD. This ushered in the Shilla Dynasty.

## The Shilla Dynasty

The next two and a half centuries (from 668 to 935) were known as the Shilla Dynasty or the Unified Kingdoms period. This marked a time of great cultural achievement for Korea; the expansion of Buddhism served as the impetus for the construction of numerous temples and the creation of great works of art.

The Shilla society was similar in some respects to western feudalism, with a large population of serf-like commoners supporting an aristocratic minority. The discontent fueled by this model of culture eventually resulted in northern warlords amassing great power and conquering Shilla from the inside, founding a new kingdom known as the Goryeo or Koryo.

## The Koryo Period

The Koryo period (from which Korea's English name was derived) lasted from the early 10th century until 1392. This period saw an increase in the centralization and power of the Korean government as well as more formal codification of the laws, the introduction of a civil service system and the spread of Buddhism throughout the entire country.

In 1231 the Mongols invaded Korea, forcing the royal family into exile and eventual surrender. For the next 150 years, the Koryo kingdom continued to exist under the control of the Mongols.

In 1392, the Korean general Yi was sent to China to fight the Ming Dynasty. He instead allied with the Chinese and returned to Korea to overthrow the existing Korean king and put himself in power, ushering in the Yi Dynasty.

## The Yi Dynasty

The Yi Dynasty, which lasted from 1392 until 1910, saw several changes in Korean culture. In 1394 Yi moved the capital of Korea to Hanyang-gun (known today as Seoul) and adopted Confucianism as Korea's state religion, causing a drastic reduction in the power of the Buddhists. In 1446, King Sejong the Great introduced the Korean alphabet, Hangul, in an effort to promote literacy among the citizenry (prior to this Koreans used Chinese Hanja for written communication; the complexity of this system limited literacy to scholars and nobles).

Japanese and western traders approached Korea in the 19th century, and Korea, fearing that an influx of foreign trade would damage its own cultural integrity, closed its borders. However, in 1876 the Japanese were able to force several disadvantageous trade agreements on Korea, eventually leading to Japan's annexation of Korea in 1910.

## Modern Korea

Japan occupied Korea from 1910 to 1945. During this time the Japanese made a concerted effort to replace Korean culture with Japanese culture. Korean citizens were forced to adopt Japanese names and adhere to the tenets of Shinto (the native Japanese religion) and were not allowed to use the Korean language. Dissension on the part of the Koreans was violently and brutally repressed.

Japan's surrender on August 15th, 1945 at the end of World War II resulted in the Korean peninsula coming under divided rule, with the USSR occupying the northern part of the peninsula, and the US occupying the south. In 1948, the UN established a democratic government, the Republic of Korea, in South Korea, with its capital in Seoul, while the Communists established the Democratic People's Republic of Korea in North Korea, with its capital in Pyongyang. In 1950, the North Korean Army invaded South Korea, starting the Korean War. This war lasted for three years and resulted in millions of casualties on both sides.

Since the end of the war in 1953, South Korea's government has gone through a series of Republics alternating between democratic, military and autocratic rule. The Sixth Republic (begun in 1983 and continuing through the writing of this book) established South Korea as a liberal democracy that has developed substantially both economically and culturally. South Korea is now one of the wealthiest nations in the world.

## *History of the Martial Arts from Which Kyuki-Do Was Developed*

Because Kyuki-Do incorporates elements of Tae Kwon Do, Judo, Jiu Jitsu and Hapkido, it is important that the dedicated student be familiar with the background and origin of these core arts.

### History of Tae Kwon Do

Tae Kwon Do can be traced back to the art of T'ae-Kyon, a kicking style that dates back to the Shilla Dynasty. Shilla was originally the smallest of the three kingdoms, and its people had to defend themselves against constant incursions from the Koguryo and the Paekche. For this reason, King Chin-Hung of the Shilla Kingdom organized the Hwarang youth group, a military organization comprised of the noble youths of the kingdom who were trained in hand-to-hand fighting techniques derived from the original T'ae-Kyon.

The Hwarang combined the spirit and honor of the warrior with the intellect and creativity of the scholar and were instrumental in the eventual unification of the three kingdoms. However, after the end of the Shilla Dynasty, T'ae-Kyon entered a period of stagnancy. During the Yi Dynasty, the Koreans focused on the importance of literary and scholarly pursuits rather than martial endeavors; as a result, T'ae-Kyon saw little development or refinement during the 600 years of the Yi Dynasty.

During the Japanese occupation of Korea, martial arts techniques from both China and Japan were introduced to the country. These martial arts relied much more heavily on hand techniques. The Koreans incorporated elements of these new styles into traditional T'ae-Kyon and taught the resulting style under a variety of names such as Tang-Su, Kong-Su, Karate, Kwon-Pop and T'ae-Su.

After the Korean liberation in 1945, there was a strong push to develop a national Korean martial art and to determine the proper name for this art. In 1955 a special board of martial arts masters, historians and prominent leaders was formed to address this problem. The board voted that the art should be described as Tae Kwon Do (the Way of the Hand and Foot). The reasons behind this selection included the close connection with T'ae Kyon in both pronunciation and meaning and the fact that the name was more appropriate than choices such as Tang-Su Do (the Way of the China Hand) or Karate (Empty Hand) given that the art employed both hand and foot techniques. The Korean Taekwondo Association (KTA) was founded in 1959 in order to promote the teaching of Tae Kwon Do as a unified system, but different schools or *kwans* continued to teach varying styles of the art. The KTA eventually came under the leadership of General Choi Hong-Hi, the man widely recognized as the father of modern Tae Kwon Do. General Choi eventually went on to found the International Taekwondo Federation (ITF) in 1966.

### History of Yudo/Judo

Yudo, the Korean form of Judo, originated over 1400 years ago (560 AD) as part of the combat training of the Hwarang warriors. In all likelihood, the original Yudo techniques were derived from a much older Chinese system brought to Korea during the Three Kingdoms period. The techniques of Yudo were originally used by the Hwarang youth group, but during the Koryo Dynasty they were modified into a form of recreation and competition.

Korean Yudo was formalized during the Yi Dynasty and was probably introduced to Japan during the Yimjin Conflict in 1592 AD; Japanese Jiu Jitsu (a general term that refers to a variety of different types of traditional Japanese fighting styles) was influenced by early Korean Yudo techniques as well as various Chinese fighting systems.

Contemporary Judo was developed in Japan during the late 1800s by Professor Jigaro Kano. Professor Kano studied under several different Jiu Jitsu masters and took what he believed to be the most effective techniques and combined them into his own style. In 1882, Professor Kano opened the Kodokan and began teaching the style that he named Judo (the Gentle Way). Professor Kano emphasized the importance of sound scientific principles in the development of proper technique and integrated a philosophy of respect, camaraderie and social welfare into the art.

During the early 1900s Judo was popularized throughout Asia; by 1911 secondary schools in Japan had adopted it as part of their students' regular physical education regimen. Judo was brought to the United States in 1902 by President Theodore Roosevelt, who, after witnessing a demonstration, imported a Japanese instructor to give him lessons. Today, Judo is an immensely popular sport throughout the world and was, until recently, the only martial art that was included in the Olympics.

Modern Judo primarily utilizes throws, pins and a variety of choking and joint-locking techniques, but traditional Judo as taught by Professor Kano was a complete art that also included striking, self-defense and resuscitation.

## History of Brazilian Jiu Jitsu

Brazilian Jiu Jitsu (commonly referred to as BJJ) is a sport and competition-based art derived from Kodokan Judo and popularized by the Gracie family. BJJ traces its roots back to 1917, when Carlos Gracie began studying Judo under the tutelage of Mitsudo Maeda, one of Jigaro Kano's top students who was tasked by Kano with traveling overseas to demonstrate and spread the art of Judo.

Carlos Gracie studied under Maeda for several years, eventually passing his knowledge on to his brothers. It was Carlos's brother Helio who modified and adapted Maeda's teachings into what is now recognized as modern BJJ.

Brazilian Jiu Jitsu is predominantly a ground-based system of fighting that emphasizes the use of locking and choking submission techniques. In recent years it has become wildly popular and forms the basis of many competitive mixed martial arts styles.

## History of Hapkido

Hapkido (the Way of Coordinated or Internal Energy) was founded by Choi Yong Sul (1904-1986). Choi Yong Sul was a native-born Korean who, when he was eight years old, was kidnapped and taken to Japan by a Japanese merchant. Choi escaped from his captor and survived by begging in the streets of Osaka. He was eventually sent to a Buddhist temple and from there to work as a servant at the home of Takeda Sokaku, a master of the Daito-ryu school of Aiki-Jujutsu. According to Choi, he studied extensively under Master Takeda until Takeda's suicide in 1943, at which point he returned to Korea. It should be noted that Choi's claims of training with Tokeda are unsubstantiated and viewed by many historians as either exaggerated or entirely falsified.

In Korea, Choi and his family supported themselves as farmers. In 1948, Choi was waiting in line to purchase grain from a brewery when several men attempted to take his place. Choi defended himself effortlessly against these men, earning the respect and admiration of Suh Bok Sup, the manager of the brewery, who was himself a first-degree black belt in Judo. Suh Bok Sup asked Choi to train him in the martial arts, and the two eventually opened a dojang together in 1951.

Over the course of the next several years, Choi's martial art was further developed and modified by the experience and outside training that his students brought to the school. Choi called his art by several different names before finally settling on Hapkido.

Hapkido is a complete martial art that incorporates kicks, strikes, blocks and deflections with joint locks, takedowns and pain compliance or pressure point techniques. It is similar in certain regards to the Japanese art of Aikido (the founder of Aikido, Ueshiba Morihei, was a contemporary of Choi who also studied Daito-ryu Aiki-Jujutsu under Takeda) but incorporates more linear, hard-style techniques.

## *History and Symbolism of the Flags*

The American Kyuki-Do Federation recommends that each school fly three flags at the front of the classroom. Each school flies the national flag of its home country to demonstrate patriotism and an understanding of our obligations to our country and community, the Korean flag to demonstrate an appreciation and respect for the cultural origin of our art, and the Federation flag to demonstrate our solidarity with the Federation and with the other practitioners of Kyuki-Do.

The following sections of the handbook will briefly describe the history and symbolism associated with each of these flags.

### The American Flag

On June 14th, 1777, the Second Continental Congress passed the Flag Resolution, which was the first official recognition of the American flag. At the time, the flag featured thirteen stars on a blue background, and thirteen red and white stripes; the stars and stripes represented the thirteen original colonies.

As additional states entered the union, additional stars and stripes were added to the flag. It was eventually decided that in order to keep the design of the flag uncluttered new stars would be added to represent each state, but that the flag would always contain thirteen stripes in recognition of the thirteen original colonies. The current design of the flag includes fifty stars and thirteen stripes.

When the flag was first created, there was no particular symbolism attached to the colors that were chosen. Meanings were attached to the colors on June 20th, 1782 when the Great Seal of the United States was defined. Red is intended to signify hardiness and valor; white signifies innocence and purity; blue signifies vigilance, perseverance and justice.

The stars and stripes, in addition to representing the colonies and states, have further meaning. The star is a symbol of the heavens, divinity and the aspiration to greatness; the stripe is representative of rays of light emanating from the sun. The original design of the flag (with thirteen stars arranged in a circle) was intended to signify the creation of a new constellation, with no single star (or colony) above another.

**Respect for the American Flag**

(Public law 94-344, 94th Congress) Resolved by the Senate and House of Representatives of the United States of America in Congress assembled. That Public Law Numbered 829, approved December 22$^{nd}$, 1942, entitled "Joint resolution to codify and emphasize existing rules and customs pertaining to the display and use of the flag of the United States of America."

The lettered paragraphs that appear below are reproduced from Title 36, Chapter 10, Section 176 of the United States Code, entitled "Respect for flag."

(b) The flag should never touch anything beneath it, such as the ground, the floor, water, or merchandise.
(d) The flag should never be used as wearing apparel, bedding, or drapery.
(g) The flag should never have placed upon it, nor any part of it, nor attached to it any mark, insignia, letter, word, figure, design, picture, or drawing of any nature.
(i) The flag should never be used for advertising purposes in any manner whatsoever. It should never be embroidered on such articles as cushions or handkerchiefs and the like, printed or otherwise impressed on paper napkins or boxes or anything that is designed for temporary use and discard.
(j) No part of the flag should ever be used as a costume or athletic uniform. However, a flag patch may be affixed to the uniform of military personnel, firemen, policemen, and members of patriotic organizations. The flag represents a living country and is itself considered a living thing.
(k) The flag, when it is in such condition that it is no longer a fitting emblem for display, should be destroyed in a dignified way, preferably by burning.

**Hanging the American Flag**

The American Flag should be hung to the left of any other displayed flags, at the same level or higher. The American flag should be the same size (or larger) than any other flags being flown alongside it.

When displayed (either horizontally or vertically), the stars of the flag should be in the upper left hand corner as seen by the viewer:

## The Korean Flag

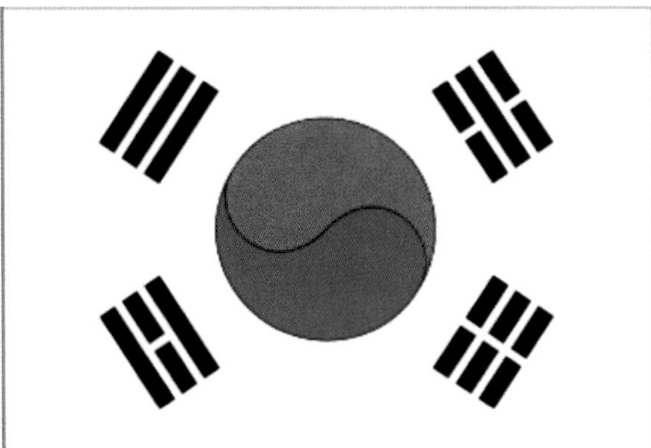

The modern version of the Korean flag was formally adopted March 6$^{th}$, 1883, during the reign of King Gojong. The flag embodies much of the philosophy of early eastern religions, as well as the intense national pride of the Korean people. The chief symbol (and sometimes the flag itself) is called Taeguk.

The Taeguk shows a white background, which symbolizes peace. Depicted in the center of the flag is a circle divided into two balanced sections; the red, high section, Yang, expresses the positive elements of the universe, while the blue, lower section, Eum or Yin, expresses the negative. Eum and Yang represent the dualism of the cosmos and embody the idea that while there is constant movement within the sphere of infinity, there is also balance and harmony. In the context of the flag, the Eum Yang represents unity and creative force.

The four Kua, or trigrams, in the corners of the flag symbolize (in clockwise order starting from the upper left) Heaven (Geon), Water (Gam), Earth (Gon) and Fire (Li). When viewed in pairs, these trigrams demonstrate additional meaning: the Fire and Water trigrams mean Light, and the Heaven and Earth trigrams mean Eternity.

The Korean flag can therefore be taken to symbolize five philosophical ideals: Peace, Unity, Creativity, Light and Eternity.

## The American Kyuki-Do Federation Flag

The American Kyuki-Do Federation flag depicts the AKF symbol on a white background with a red and blue border. Written at the bottom of the flag are the words "American Kyuki-Do Federation." The Hanja (or ideograms) at the top spell out "Mee Guk Kyuki-Do Hyup Pae," which is Korean for "American Kyuki-Do Federation."

The AKF symbol is a closed fist covered by an open hand, with the Eum Yang in the background. The name of the Federation is written at the top, and the hanja for "Kyuki-Do" are written at the bottom. The meaning of the AKF symbol is discussed in detail in the next section of the handbook.

# Chapter Two: Philosophy and Conduct

Kyuki-Do is much more than a simple sport or method of self-defense, and it requires more of the student than mere exercise and practice. Kyuki-Do teaches us a way of life; it teaches us how to be good in addition to how to be strong and healthy. The following sections of the handbook provide details on the type of conduct that is expected from the practitioners of our art.

## *The Philosophy and Symbolism of Kyuki-Do*

Each student joins Kyuki-Do for different reasons, hoping to gain something different from it. Some people join for practical reasons such as physical fitness or the desire to learn self-defense. Others join in order to develop discipline, self-confidence and self-esteem. Still others join simply out of curiosity about the martial arts. There is no single, unifying purpose common to all students, and there doesn't need to be; Kyuki-Do offers different things to different people. That is one of the great strengths of the art.

Kyuki-Do can be seen as a method or vehicle for the attainment of the student's unique physical, mental and spiritual goals. Kyuki-Do provides dedicated practitioners with the impetus, the drive, the spirit and the fortitude to forge themselves into the people they want to be. It is neither a simple system of training and techniques intended to make people into outstanding fighters, nor is it a religion or philosophy that seeks to impose its own truths on the student; rather it is a tool that students can use to find the strength to achieve their goals while acting in accordance with their own personal philosophy or spirituality.

This is useless, however, unless the student has clear goals that he or she is striving to achieve and a personal philosophy by which he or she is abiding. Too many people drift through their lives with no sense of purpose, with no idea of what they should do, with no guiding philosophy to help them make sense of their lives.

It is therefore necessary for each student to have a purpose or dream or goal to strive toward and a personal philosophy to guide them on their path. This is true of all students, both young and old, but it is especially important for young people today.

Youth is a powerful time, full of energy, fire, life and potential. If this energy can be focused, it becomes a powerful force, capable of helping the student attain great things. However, if the energy of youth is not focused, it is wasted, or worse, it becomes misapplied toward inappropriate or destructive goals.

For this reason, each student should strive to do the following:

- Develop a personal philosophy
- Determine their personal goals
- Use the teachings of Kyuki-Do and the strength of character developed through martial arts training to achieve their goals while remaining true to their personal philosophy

It should again be stressed that Kyuki-Do is not, in and of itself, a religion or a system of spirituality. Kyuki-Do is a tool for personal growth that is compatible with each student's own religious, moral or spiritual background. Kyuki-Do strives to teach the student certain basic elements of moral behavior (such as the Tenets), but the art's primary purpose lies not in teaching a set of moral rules, but rather in helping the practitioner develop the wisdom to determine right from wrong on their own, and the strength of character to always choose what is right.

## Purpose of Kyuki-Do

The purpose of Kyuki-Do is to create individuals who are physically and mentally progressive and productive, and who are aware of their physical, mental and moral obligations to themselves and others. The idea underlying this purpose is that each student of Kyuki-Do should strive to do their best for the good of all.

The ultimate goal of Kyuki-Do is to spark the growth and development of the spirit, mind and body and to encourage contribution for the greater good of society. This means that the student of Kyuki-Do should not be concerned with comparing themselves to others, but rather with continuously working toward becoming a better person.

## Eum and Yang

The Chinese Yin Yang (called Eum Yang in Korean) is a visual and linguistic depiction of reality. It is simultaneously a practical and theoretical guide to understanding the nature of the universe as it **is** rather than as the individual believes that it **should be**. It is a symbol that reflects the totality of the universe as a well-coordinated and balanced system in which everything is related to everything else.

The Eum and Yang interact and exist both in harmony and opposition, as complimentary and contradictory forces. These forces compose the totality of the universe and exist only relative to each other. For example, the concept of "positive" (Yang) cannot exist, have meaning or be defined without the existence of the opposing concept of "negative" (Eum). "Long" (Yang) cannot exist or be understood without "short" (Eum). Other examples of Yang and Eum include old/young, hard/soft, mind/body, life/death, water/fire, earth/sky. None of these concepts can exist or be understood except in relation to their opposites. This duality is expressed in every aspect of the universe.

As a theory of reality, the Eum Yang focuses on process, order and universal laws of operation. Eum and Yang represent existence as a dynamic process of change that obeys definite universal laws, follows definite patterns and is based on pre-established harmony.

Eum and Yang are also apparent in human nature and behavior. The balance of destruction and creativity, of hope and despair and of good and bad within each individual reflects the philosophy of Eum and Yang that is embodied in Kyuki-Do. Kyuki-Do recognizes the dual qualities that are contained within each person and assists the individual in improving the inner balance of their mind, body, spirit and emotions. The goal is to direct the student to make full use of themselves in more positive and productive ways.

Eum and Yang also tells us that no person can be either completely good or completely bad. In even the most dedicated, peaceful, humble and compassionate individual, there still exists the potential for laziness, arrogance and cruelty; therefore, each of us must always be alert to the possibility that we may succumb to these flaws. Similarly, even the most deeply flawed people still have within them the capacity for good; it is therefore our responsibility to seek out and cultivate that potential.

The student of Kyuki-Do is encouraged to explore their potential and recognize the positive characteristics within. The student is then able to utilize these attributes to the maximum benefit of both the individual and of society in general. The student also recognizes their shortcomings and so develops a more realistic approach to life.

On a much larger scale, Kyuki-Do helps the individual to know, recognize and appreciate human values and human potentials both physically and mentally. Through Kyuki-Do and the philosophy of Eum and Yang, students will improve their internal and external balance and their relationship with the world around them.

## The Symbol of Kyuki-Do

Kyuki-Do is symbolized by a closed fist and an open palm perpendicular to each other. The open hand symbolizes good and peace, as well as a strong and healthy mind, developed through adherence to the tenets and philosophy of Kyuki-Do. The closed fist symbolizes power, as well as a strong and healthy body, developed through the physical training of Kyuki-Do. The open hand and closed fist are held together by the spirit of the individual; this spirit brings the mental and the physical together to create harmony within each of us. Kyuki-Do tempers the spirit within us and encourages us to continue to strive and persevere through adversity and accept our successes with humility. The symbol reflects the harmonious survival of opposites both within ourselves and within the world in which we live.

The outline of the Kyuki-Do symbol is in the shape of a keyhole. When you look at an object through a keyhole, you must totally focus in order to see it clearly. The message behind the shape of the symbol is that you must totally focus on the development of your martial arts skills in order to gain a true understanding and insight into the nature and purpose of Kyuki-Do.

## Mind Body Spirit

Kyuki-Do strives to awaken each student's spiritual, mental and physical potential. It is important that each student attain a balance between Ma Eum (Mind), Mohm (Body) and Jung Shin (Spirit). Training and developing one or two of these three areas at the expense of the others will hinder the student's development.

Ma Eum (Mind): The student must be attentive, alert and eager to receive new information and new instruction. No matter how strong the body or the spirit, a student who fails to continually develop their mental capabilities will eventually stagnate and fail to progress in their training. A student who is weak in mind will not have the ability to understand how to properly apply their technique.

Mohm (Body): The student must continually strive for physical fitness and good health. They must continually seek to become stronger, faster and better conditioned. While a strong mind is essential to the understanding of proper technique, if the body is weak or unhealthy, technique cannot be properly applied. A student who is weak in body will not have the stamina or strength to effectively execute technique.

Jung Shin (Spirit): The student must always work toward becoming a better person. They must live a life filled with humility, integrity and compassion toward others. While a strong mind and a strong body will allow a student to develop superior martial arts skills, a strong spirit is necessary to ensure that those skills are used in a manner that benefits humanity as a whole. A student who is weak in spirit may become arrogant, selfish or violent.

## Who I Am

The patterns from the forms Kibon (✚), Kicho (T) and Kyuki Il Chang (⊥) when superimposed over each other create the following Chinese character:

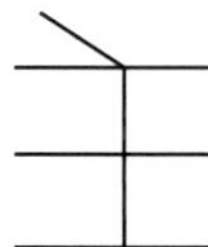

In Chinese, this character is pronounced "Ju" and means the "True You," defined as a person who is spiritually, mentally and physically strong; someone who has a clear vision and purpose and whose life choices consistently fulfill that vision and purpose. In other words, such a person is living life with purpose and meaning, without any pretense, and accepting all responsibility.

Of the three horizontal lines, the top line represents the spiritual (heaven), the middle line represents the mental (people or mind) and the bottom line represents the physical (earth or body). The vertical line that connects the three horizontal lines represents your hopes, dreams and desires and your purpose and direction in life. The diagonal line at the top indicates your indomitable spirit and perseverance. The Chinese character for king is the character above without the diagonal line at the top and means that you are the king or ruler of your own destiny. It also indicates willpower, strength of character, and a strong focus and purpose.

## *Student Conduct*

Kyuki-Do is more than merely a physical discipline; it is a philosophy that endeavors to make its practitioners into better people. For this reason, it is expected that students of Kyuki-Do should always conduct themselves in an honorable and appropriate manner, both within the dojang and during their day-to-day life. Students are expected to understand and abide by the Student Pledge and the Tenets of Kyuki-Do, as well as all of the rules and bylaws of the American Kyuki-Do Federation and their individual dojang.

### The Student Pledge

All Kyuki-Do participants, from student to instructor to Master, must commit themselves to high behavioral and moral standards of excellence. Each participant is expected to learn and adhere to five ideals beneficial to their personal growth in Kyuki-Do. They pledge to conduct themselves accordingly both at the dojang and in their daily life. Through this personal commitment, the student of Kyuki-Do will improve the relationship between their own mind, body and spirit, as well as their relationship with the world around them.

I) I shall respect my instructor and all senior ranks.
II) I shall conduct myself in a respectful manner.
III) I shall respect the teachings of Kyuki-Do and never misuse them.
IV) I shall always respect the rights of others.
V) I shall strive for peace and camaraderie in the world.

### The Tenets of Kyuki-Do

A tenet is simply a principle, opinion or school of thought maintained by an individual or organization that provides direction toward an established goal. The six tenets of Kyuki-Do are as follows:

- Courtesy: Treating people with the respect, no matter their station in life.
- Humility: Recognizing that no matter how great your accomplishments are, they do not make you a better person than anyone else.
- Integrity: Knowing the difference between right and wrong, and choosing to do what is right. Being whole and living a true life by adhering to your principles and goals.
- Perseverance: Continuing even in the face of adversity.
- Self-Control: Exercising restraint over yourself, and being in command of your thoughts, feelings and actions.
- Indomitable Spirit: The spark that gives you the power to persevere. Having faith in what you do and knowing that if you are traveling a worthwhile path, eventually success and achievement will be realized.

Through practice and application of these tenets, the Kyuki-Do student gains increased self-confidence and motivation, as well as the capacity and desire to improve their own life and the lives of those around them.

## General Rules for the Kyuki-Do Student

I) Every student should always seek truth and practice it.
II) Every student should promote moral behavior and good character, both in themselves and in others.
III) Every student should respect and obey their parents, teachers and seniors.
IV) Every student should love and respect their country and contribute to their community.
V) Every student should strive to develop both confidence and humility, and practice both at all times.
VI) Every student should do their best to promote intellectuality.
VII) Every student should be willing to sacrifice their own interests for justice.
VIII) Every student should do their utmost to support, promote and develop Kyuki-Do, as well as the Federation and the school.
IX) Every student should develop their physical, mental and spiritual endurance.
X) Every student should always remember that the purpose of Kyuki-Do is to promote both mental and physical health.

## Dojang Rules and Etiquette

Note that the following is provided as an example of Dojang rules; different academies are likely to have different protocol. All academies will expect their student to be respectful and courteous.

I) Entering the Dojang:
   a. When stepping onto the mats, students must pause and bow.
II) Starting Class: Each school will follow their own bow-in. Generally:
   a. All grade holders (yukupja) shall line up facing the instructor.
   b. All black belt holders (yudanja) shall line up on the side at the front of class to the instructor's right.
   c. During the salutations at the beginning and end of the class, only the head instructor of the school shall take the place at the front center of the class. An exception would be when a guest instructor from another school is present.
   d. The highest ranking grade holder (yukupja) will call out the salutation:
      i. Charyot! Kukiyeh daehaiyo kyung-nyeh. (Attention! Salute to the flag.)
      ii. Paro. (Return)
      iii. Charyot! Sahbum-nim daehaiyo kyung-nyeh. (Attention! Bow to the instructor.)

iv. Yudanja daehaiyo kyung-nyeh. (Bow to the black belts.)

e. At this point, the instructor may give the command to kneel and meditate.

III) During Class:

a. During class, proper respect and discipline must be shown at all times.
b. Address all senior ranks with appropriate respect.
c. Be punctual. If circumstances arise requiring you to be late, please call ahead. Chronic unexcused tardiness will result in discipline.
d. When a student comes to class late, they should wait until recognized by the instructor, bow and request permission to join the class.
e. When a student must leave class during training, They should first receive permission from the instructor.
f. After leaving the mat, students should ask for permission before returning.
g. Students should follow all class instructions implicitly.
h. Anything that would prevent the student from performing in class to their fullest should be discussed with the instructor prior to class.
i. No food or drink is allowed on the mats. No gum should be chewed during class.
j. Remove your shoes and socks before stepping on the mats.
k. No jewelry is to be worn in class, with the exception of unadorned wedding bands. If students have piercings that can be removed, they must be removed prior to class. Piercings that cannot be removed should be carefully taped over.
l. There should be an absence of unnecessary noise in the dojang. Students should remain silent, especially during forms and free-fighting. Cell phones should be silenced while class is in session.
m. Students on the sidelines should remain still so as not to disturb those who are currently practicing or training.
n. While seated, students should keep a proper posture. A kneeling or seated position with the legs crossed in front is acceptable.
o. Younger students must show respect to their seniors, regardless of rank.
p. Students and instructors are encouraged to use Korean terminology in the dojang.
q. Always use appropriate and respectful language. There is no place in the school for cursing, swearing, speaking out of turn or using inappropriate words or phrases.
r. Fingernails and toenails should be kept short and neatly trimmed in order to prevent injury to self and others.

IV) Dismissing the Class: Each school will follow their own bow-in. Generally:

a. All grade holders (yukupja) shall line up facing the instructor.
b. All black belt holders (yudanja) shall line up on the side at the front of class to the instructor's right.
c. The instructor may give the command to kneel and meditate.
d. The highest ranking grade holder (yukupja) will call out the salutation:
    i. Charyot! Kukiyeh daehaiyo kyung-nyeh. (Attention! Salute to the flag.)
    ii. Paro. (Return)

iii. Charyot! Sahbum-nim daehaiyo kyung-nyeh. (Attention! Bow to the instructor.)
iv. Yudanja daehaiyo kyung-nyeh. (Bow to the black belts.)

e. The students may shake each others' hands and line up at the front of class.
f. The instructor will dismiss the class.

V) Leaving the Dojang:
a. When stepping off the mats, students must pause and bow.

VI) The Uniform (Dobok) and Belt (Dee):
a. Students should always keep their dobok clean and in good repair.
b. The lapels of the uniform should be crossed left over right.
c. The belt should be tied in a square knot in the front, and the ends should be of even length.
d. The uniform and belt should always be worn properly before, during and after class.
e. When not in use, the uniform and belt should be carefully and respectfully folded or hung up.
f. Face away from the flags, students and instructors when tying your belt or adjusting your uniform.
g. Any patches or insignia on the uniform should be arranged as follows:
i. Left lapel: School patch
ii. Right lapel: Federation patch
iii. Left shoulder: Korean flag patch
iv. Right shoulder: American flag patch
h. Always wear your uniform to class. If you do not have a uniform, wear comfortable, loose-fitting clothes.
i. For formal AKF events, students should wear whatever uniform is specified by the AKF for that event.

Always remain respectful of the school, the equipment and especially the other students and instructors. Learning martial arts should be an enjoyable experience, but always remember that your actions and attitude within the school reflect on your instructor and fellow students as well as on yourself.

# Chapter Three: Training

This section of the handbook will address what the new student can expect during each class and how they can maximize the benefits that they will receive from their training.

## *Beginning Your Kyuki-Do Training*

We expect our students to show respect for the history and teachings of Kyuki-Do at all times. This means that each and every student becomes an emissary of the art; we should never do anything in our everyday life that is not representative of a true martial artist.

Like all martial arts, Kyuki-Do requires of its students a great deal of devotion and commitment. It demands continuous practice and a sense of perfectionism. The student should therefore cultivate the following four attributes:

I) Willingness to learn.
II) Determination to achieve their goals, physical, mental and spiritual.
III) Willingness to practice alone on a daily basis outside of class.
IV) Complete cooperation with their instructors and classmates.

The student is expected to maintain proper discipline and attitude whenever he or she is in the dojang. Complete obedience to the instructor is a must. Respect for higher ranks and bowing before entering the dojang are requirements. Discipline should always be the fundamental attitude of each student and the most prominent characteristic observed in viewing a class. Rough-housing in the training area before or after class, excessive and loud talking, chewing gum, swearing and whistling are all strictly prohibited. The emphasis on self-control in the training area will eventually develop into a strong sense of discipline, which will carry over into every facet of the student's life.

The dojang is where one comes to learn humbleness and obedience, respect and good manners. It is where one observes leadership and commitment, friendship and unity. It is where one becomes not only physically tired, but also mentally strong and energetic.

As in other sports, the first days are particularly hard and may seem to be discouraging, particularly if one compares oneself to other students in class; it is important to note that many of the students at the school have been training for months or even years. It is to be expected that there will be a substantial disparity in skill and fitness between the beginning student and the established student. One should look to one's fellow classmates as examples of what one should strive to accomplish, but it is important that the beginning student not be discouraged by the difference between their fitness level and that of their classmates.

During the first classes, the student will be obliged to use and exercise different parts of the body that may have been dormant for years, resulting in pain and aches all over the body. It is natural for the muscles to respond negatively to the new and unusual movements found in martial arts techniques. The first days become more challenging and more difficult as one tries to teach and train the muscles for a particular movement or exercise; to keep pace with the exercise is a burden that requires not only physical endurance, but mental strength as well. The obstacles of the first days encourage strength and growth; they are the building blocks by which the student develops and matures physically and mentally as a responsible martial artist.

The new student is advised to slowly develop and adapt to the new exercises. The student is encouraged to do his or her best at his or her own pace. The training of Kyuki-Do emphasizes ongoing personal improvement rather than the attainment of specific fitness goals.

The new student should spend considerable time stretching and loosening up in the early stages of practice. One should also work on coordination and balance by repeatedly practicing basic kicking and blocking techniques. The basic forms are one of the best methods of learning coordination and concentration when practiced regularly and thoroughly. The student is encouraged to learn forms and practice them as often as possible. A thorough understanding of these different exercises and techniques and a complete commitment to the martial arts will make the early days much more enjoyable and useful.

The student should develop a daily exercise program that is acceptable to one's body and one's schedule. It is recommended that, to maintain fitness, one should work out at least three times per week. To gain fitness, one should work out four to six times per week. The exercise should be at least fifteen minutes long. Working out six days a week for fifteen or twenty minutes will be more beneficial than two one-hour workouts a week.

## Developing Your Personal Workout Routine

- One should start with relaxing the upper body, using movements such as trunk rotations, side stretches, etc. Then do your aerobic and power exercises, such as push-ups, sit-ups, jogging, jumping jacks, rope-jumping and so forth. Finish with the leg stretches.
- When stretching the neck avoid rotating the neck in a circular motion. Stretch the neck by bringing it forward, then back, then side to side. Avoid sharp, snapping movements that could strain the neck or cause injury to the vertebrae.
- When performing leg stretches, such as the hamstring stretches, stretch forward slowly and bend at the waist to prevent stress on the lower back. To aid in doing this try to touch your chin to your knee, not the forehead.
- Avoid ballistic stretching. This means avoid bouncing the head to the knee. When you bounce, you can pull muscles more easily.
- Make sure to warm up properly before kicking to avoid pulling the major muscles in the leg. A pulled hamstring can take up to six weeks to heal.
- Do not overdo your exercise. Progress gradually to the level that you want to be at and remember that over-exerting yourself may cause injuries that will dramatically hamper your ability to attain your fitness goals.

## *The Bow (Kyung-nyeh)*

The bow can be perceived in many different ways and has a variety of meanings or purposes. The bow can be a statement of greeting or departure. It can show respect or appreciation. It can define a certain position of status or rank. The bow can show honor or express apology.

Whenever the student enters or leaves the dojang they bow. Whenever they greet their instructor or fellow students they bow. If the student must leave the class momentarily they bow upon leaving and returning. When they face each other for sparring they first bow to each other, and again when they finish sparring. Prior to performing the hyungs, they bow. In tournament competition there are pre-established times when and where the student will bow. Martial arts tradition demands that they bow in all of these circumstances. Therefore, the bow or kyung-nyeh must be considered a standard preliminary. The bow shows respect to your instructor, to your fellow students and to the training hall. The bow also demonstrates your humility, character and black belt attitude and should never be disregarded.

### Protocol for Bowing and Shaking Hands

There are basically three different types of bows. The first type is the shallow bow (mostly the shoulders and head) that shows the respect of the parent to the child, the instructor to the student, or the student to another student. It is proper for all students to bow in this manner during sparring or partner drills. A deeper bow (from the waist) shows the greater respect of the child to the parent or the student to the instructor. It is proper for all students to bow in this manner when in class and while testing or competing in front of judges. The last type of bow is the kneeling bow. It was used by soldiers to the general and the king. It is used to ask for forgiveness or to show deep appreciation and respect for someone. Sometimes it is used as part of a goodbye before a long journey.

When students shake hands with the instructors at the end of class, they should shake with the right hand and support the right arm with the left hand underneath the forearm, palm facing down, by the elbow.This is an honorable way to show respect and express appreciation. They may say “kamsahamnida,” which means “thank you very much.” This is expressed first by the student and then answered by the instructor in the same manner.

## *Meditation*

Meditation is a relaxed yet focused state of mind developed through certain breathing and relaxation methods. When one meditates, the eyes should be closed to decrease external distractions.

In Kyuki-Do, there is no religious significance attached to meditation. It is used solely to relax and practice breathing patterns. Learning to breathe properly is often neglected; most people use only a third or a half of their lung capacity and consequently lose much potential energy. One's body and blood need oxygen to function properly, or else one will tire easily when working, playing or exercising. Meditation helps one focus on proper breathing patterns and trains the body to breathe fully and deeply.

Each class may begin and end with a moment of meditation and personal reflection. Meditation before class allows the student to clear the mind of any distractions and mentally prepare for the workout ahead. The student should concentrate on maintaining proper attitude and etiquette during practice.

Meditation after class allows the student to concentrate on what they learned and what techniques need improvement. This should be a time for reflection, when the students mentally ask themselves "Did I put forth my best effort or could I have tried harder?" "Do I feel better about myself now as compared to before class?" Oftentimes, after a satisfying workout the student leaves the dojang better able to handle the stresses of their personal life.

Meditation will strengthen mental control; this in turn improves physical performance. If your mind is not focused solely on the workout, it will show in your performance. Mental preparation before a workout or competition and self-evaluation afterwards are vital in building a closer relationship between the mind and body. This is the purpose of meditation as well as the goal of Kyuki-Do.

## *Kihap*

Literally translated, **"Ki"** means energy and **"Hap"** means to bring together. The kihap is a short, deep, explosive sound, generated from the diaphragm. It is intended to accomplish several things:

1. To concentrate your mental, physical and spiritual energy.
2. To release your tension or stress. Under stress, we have a tendency to hyper-ventilate, or breathe shallowly. A sharp yell will help you control your breathing, maintain your oxygen supply and, therefore, maintain your strength.
3. To tighten and protect your stomach. As we yell, we flatten our diaphragm by expelling air. If you are struck in the stomach as you kihap, you will not have the wind knocked out of you.
4. To startle or distract the opponent. The kihap can have a psychological effect on your opponent, possibly freezing them for a split second, giving you the element of surprise.
5. The kihap imparts extra power in your technique beyond that of silent exhalation. Studies have indicated that vocalizing while exerting force increases power output by 11% when compared to simply exhaling, and by 25% when compared to not exhaling. [1]

---

[1] Rodolico, C.; Oberholzer, R.; and Smith, S. (2014) "Effect of Vocalization on Static Handgrip Force Output," *International Journal of Exercise Science: Conference Proceedings*: Vol. 9 : Iss. 2 , Article 67.

## *Theory of Power*

The development of powerful technique is not accidental; rather it is the end result of the application of a specific set of principles. Comprehension and mastery of the following principles are integral to achieving power.

- Concentration: In order to deliver maximum force, one must exercise mental, physical and spiritual concentration:
  - Mental: The narrowing of the field of attention, the fixing of the mental eye upon a chosen object or task. When this state is achieved, the mind can command the body to fully utilize all of the principles mentioned here to perform a desired action or technique with maximum power and effectiveness.
  - Physical: Being fluid and relaxed during the transition phase of a movement and tensing the appropriate muscles at the completion of the technique; applying the force of the impact into the smallest target area and thereby concentrating the force and increasing its effect.
  - Spiritual: Focusing all of one's energy at the point of impact using the kihap (yell).
- Reaction Force: Using reciprocal action during the execution of a technique assists in maintaining balance and increasing force. When striking, the opposite side of your body should be pulled back to add power to your delivery and to maintain your balance.
- Equilibrium: Power is dependent on proper stability. If you are unstable while delivering a technique, you are likely to stumble or fall, which will absorb much of the power that you are directing at your target.
- Breath Control: Exhaling at the point of impact will tighten your muscles, flatten your stomach and increase the speed of your delivery. Additionally, proper breath control will keep you from holding your breath or hyperventilating (either of which will interfere with your ability to execute proper technique). The use of the kihap also achieves extra power greater than that of silent exhalation.
- Speed and Mass: Force is determined by mass (effectively the weight of the striking object) and acceleration (how fast the object is traveling in the intended direction). In other words, if you want to increase the power of a punch, you will need to increase mass (by putting more of your body behind the technique) and/or speed (how fast you are throwing the punch).

The student is encouraged to study and apply these theories in their techniques. **The neglect of any of these factors will result in a decrease of power.**

Proper application of the Theory of Power will only come with sufficient training and attention to proper technique:

- Training: Dedicated training and practice in Kyuki-Do will develop all of the elements contained in total physical fitness. This training will also develop the muscles used specifically for striking, kicking, throwing and grappling techniques.

- Proper Technique: Sheer muscular strength is not enough. It must be coupled with proper technique in order for optimal striking power to be achieved; the twisting the hips during a side kick or the pulling back of the left fist when executing a right punch are just two examples.

## *Strength*

Any movement requires strength and the movements inherent in the martial arts are no exception. There are two types of strength: enduring strength and explosive strength.

- **Enduring strength** (or muscle endurance) is the ability of the muscles to perform for long periods of time against small loads. Endurance exercises (such as jogging, kicking drills, hyung and sparring) are activities which help build your cardiovascular and lung capacity, as well as your enduring strength.
- **Explosive strength** is the ability of the muscles to move heavy loads rapidly. Developing explosive strength is imperative for effective martial arts and will allow you to act and react in a much more efficient way while sparring. Explosive strength can be improved through bag work (speed bag, heavy bag, focus pad), one-step sparring, practice of hand combinations, sparring and the practice of the hyungs.

## *Total Physical Fitness*

One of the goals of the true martial artist should be to develop total physical fitness. Total fitness goes beyond simple strength, speed and endurance. To be totally fit, the martial artist must master a number of different physical attributes:

- **Strength:** Strength refers both to the effort one can exert with a single maximal contraction, and to the sustained effort one can maintain over time.
- **Speed:** Speed refers to the rapidity with which successive movements can be executed.
- **Power:** Power is a combination of both strength and speed. It implies the ability to develop fast, explosive movements against resistance.
- **Neuromuscular Coordination:** This refers to the interaction between the body's nervous system and muscular system. This is required to produce skilled movements.
- **Agility:** Agility is the ability to quickly change the direction of the movement of the body.
- **Balance:** Balance refers to one's competence in maintaining their equilibrium.
- **Flexibility:** Flexibility is the range of possible motion in a joint or series of joints.
- **Heart and Breathing Muscles:** The heart is primarily a muscular pump, and the inhalation of air into the lungs takes place only as a result of the contraction of the breathing (respiratory) muscles. Both sets of muscles (heart and respiratory) get stronger only as a result of strenuous exercise that is continued for at least 15-20 minutes.
- **Controlling Fat Level:** Excess fat interferes with one's agility, speed and endurance and places an undesirable stress on the heart.
- **Body Maintenance:** Proper nutrition and adequate rest also play a vital role in developing and maintaining total physical fitness.

# Chapter Four: Application

The following chapter of the handbook provides information on the proper application of Kyuki-Do's techniques, including board-breaking, targeting and vital areas, one-step sparring and sparring.

# *Breaking*

Board breaking is done primarily to demonstrate the Theory of Power. It should never be attempted as a way to impress your friends. It is the culmination of hard study and application of the basics you are taught. In order to break, one must clear one's mind so that there are no distractions. By concentrating the mind, body and spirit into one single purpose, breaking is achieved.

One should not attempt to break without trained supervision and instructor approval. Breaking incorrectly can result in serious injuries. When your instructor feels you have enough experience and ability, they will show you the proper way.

## Physics of Breaking

A number of different elements go into a successful breaking technique. These include:

- **Force:** Any push or pull that causes an object to move or to change its speed or direction of motion. For every force there is an equal and opposite force.
- **Energy:** The ability to do work.
- **Inertia:** The resistance of objects to any change in their motion: the tendency of a body to remain in its state (at rest or in motion) until it is acted upon by an outside force.
- **Variables:** Any factors that affect the results. Harmony between the holder and technician, density of the material being broken, angle of the strike, penetration through the target, stability of the hold, proper point of contact, accurate aim of the strike or kick and proper technique.

## *Target Areas*

A **target area** refers to any sensitive area or breakable joint on the body that is vulnerable to attack. Knowing these target areas and the damaging effects of strikes, pressure or hyperextension to these areas will enable you to instantly execute a counter-attack sufficient to stun the aggressor, avoid further assault and escape.

In terms of self-defense, from whatever position you find yourself in (grabbed from behind, in a headlock, a choke or on the ground, etc.) you should be able to instantly evaluate what target areas on the opponent are open to attack, and from your position, which self-defense techniques would be most effective to use.

Depending upon the severity of the situation, any of the following methods may be used to discourage an assault:

1) Desecalation of the situation or retreat from the situation (these are always the optimal choices if feasible).
2) Injury or direct pressure/hyperextension to an area or joint that creates severe pain and/or the apprehension of more pain.
3) Immobilizing holds that will prevent further attack.
4) Injury or direct pressure to the throat or neck area that will render the attacker unconscious.
5) Extreme injury to one or more vital target areas, possibly resulting in death.

Proper strikes to the following target areas will finish or immobilize an opponent with much less energy than strikes to other areas, thus accomplishing an effective self-defense regardless of the opponent's size or strength.

- **Eyes:** Extremely sensitive to strikes, injury results in loss of function, great pain.
- **Ears:** Cupping blow increases pressure in ear canal causing rupture of eardrum. Injury affects opponent's balance and hearing.
- **Temple:** Injury stuns opponent, potential loss of conciousness.
- **Nose:** Extremely sensitive to injury, fractures, extremely vascular (bleeds easily), potential loss of consciousness. Well supplied with sensory nerves, injury causes severe pain, upward thrusting strikes very effective.
- **Chin:** Blows delivered upward very effective, potential injury to teeth, jaw and neck.
- **Jaw:** Susceptible to fracture/dislocation, injury causes severe pain.
- **Carotid Arteries:** Choking techniques that apply bilateral pressure result in rapid loss of consciousness.
- **Adam's Apple, Trachea:** An effective stun strike. Injury results in inflammation, obstructs breathing, extremely sensitive to strikes. Injury stimulates opponent's natural fear of smothering.
- **Solar Plexus:** Effective stun strike—elbow, punch or palm. Strikes or kicks to this area will interfere with opponent's breathing.

- **Ribs:** Susceptible to fracture, injury interferes with opponent's breathing. Note that the bottom (or "floating") rib is most vulnerable. Elbow and knee strikes, hand and foot techniques are effective.
- **Stomach:** Internal injury results in pain, hemorrhage.
- **Kidneys:** Strikes or kicks cause internal injury and pain.
- **Coccyx:** Susceptible to fracture, injury causes great pain and decreased mobility.
- **Groin:** Lifting or upward strikes are extremely effective, achieves stun, causes great pain.
- **Thighs:** Powerful kicks cause pain and loss of function.
- **Knees, Shins, Instep:** Susceptible to fracture, causes pain and loss of function.
- **Hair:** Pulling causes pain, allows for manipulation of the head for strikes or takedowns.
- **Shoulder:** Joint locks can cause internal injury, dislocation leads to loss of function.
- **Neck and Spine:** Injury may lead to paralysis. Kicks, strikes or manipulation are effective.
- **Elbows, Wrists, Fingers:** Susceptible to fracture. Hyperextension/rotation causes great pain, dislocation and loss of function. Allows for control of opponent.

# General Target Areas

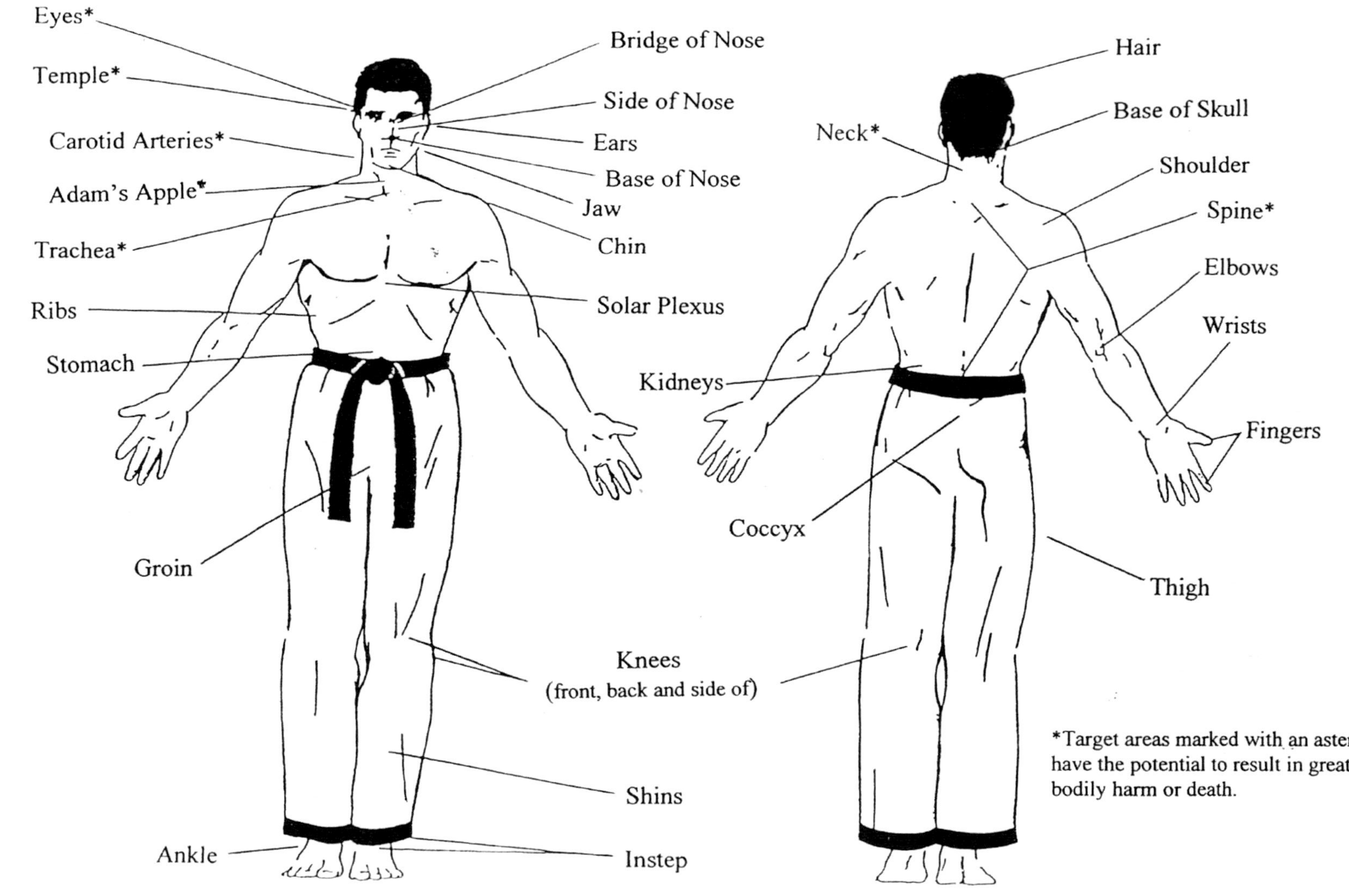

# *One-Step Sparring*

One-step sparring is a controlled situation where one student simulates being a street attacker and throws a single punch. The punch is focused at a pre-determined target, with control, and normally stepping in with the technique, the idea being that one should position oneself far enough away from the opponent to force him to commit to a technique.

This attack is received first by a movement out of range or off line, forcing the opponent to overextend and be off balance and open for a counterattack. The movement is followed by a blocking technique, coupled with a counterattack. The specific counterattack will be determined based on the size and power of the opponent. Each one-step should incorporate each of these three elements: movement, blocking and countering.

When practicing in class, the student should always exercise great control; the real battle is outside the training hall, not in it. If you injure your classmates, they will not volunteer to train with you.

The student should develop several good defenses against different angles of attack. It is better to have a select few techniques that work for you all the time than fifty that you cannot perform effectively. Your one-step techniques should be practiced so often that you are able to execute them without having to stop and think.

## Purpose of One-Step Sparring

One-step sparring develops the power and skill necessary to neutralize an attacker through the application of a single, well-placed technique or combination of techniques focused on vital areas of the target's body. It improves the student's reaction time and builds a repertoire of effective responses that the student can use should they need to defend themselves.

## Types of One-Step Sparring

- Ilbo Daeryan (One-Step Sparring): The attacker steps in with a single punch to a predetermined target (usually the head). This is the simplest type of one-step and is appropriate for all ranks.
- Ebo Daeryan (Two-Step Sparring): The attacker steps in with a single punch followed by a single kick (usually a front snap kick, but the instructor may choose to vary the specific technique based on the skill level of the students involved). This type of one-step sparring is suitable for intermediate to advanced students.
- Sambo Daeryan (Three-Step Sparring): The attacker advances while throwing three punches at the defender (usually high section, and usually one step per punch). The specific techniques and targets can be varied based on the skill level of the students involved; the instructor may, for example, have the attacker substitute a grabbing technique for the third punch. The purpose of three-step

sparring is to develop the defender's ability to effectively block and counter while retreating. This type of one-step sparring is suitable for all ranks.

- Chayu Ilbo Daeryan (Freestyle One-Step Sparring): Freestyle one-step sparring is intended to simulate the dynamic aspect of a sudden, unexpected attack. The defender faces the attacker with their hands down, simulating a worst-case scenario where they have been caught flat-footed. The attacker may attack with strikes, kicks, grabs or attempted takedowns. This type of one-step sparring is the most difficult and demanding and is most appropriate for advanced ranks.
- One-Step Sparring Variations: One-step sparring may be modified in a number of different ways. Possible variations include seated one-steps, prone one-steps, multiple attackers, limited mobility (when the defender is in a corner or against a wall) or the introduction of weapons.

## Procedure for One-Step Sparring

1. Basic one-step sparring begins with two students facing each other at attention, one arm's-length distance apart.
2. The attacker steps forward with the left foot into a back stance, and the defender steps back with the right foot into a back stance.
3. The attacker kihaps to show that he or she is prepared to attack.
4. The defender kihaps to show that he or she is prepared to receive the attack.
5. The attacker steps in and executes their attack (generally a single head-high punch, but this may be varied at the discretion of the instructor).
6. The defender moves, blocks and executes a countering technique. The defender kihaps on their final counter-technique, indicating that they are finished.
7. The attacker and defender return to left foot forward back stances.
8. The previous defender becomes the attacker for the next one-step. The students continue to alternate back and forth in this manner until the instructor calls for them to stop.

There are several important things that the student should take note of when practicing one-step sparring:

- *One-step sparring should be done with intensity.* The attack and defense are both intended to represent actual self-defense. Training with low intensity builds sloppy habits that will interfere with the student's ability to effectively apply technique should doing so ever become necessary.
- *One-steps should be kept simple.* While there is nothing wrong with practicing complicated counterattacks, always remember that basic, simple techniques are more likely to work in a real situation. Do not abandon the basics in favor of flashier, more elaborate techniques.
- *One-steps should be practiced with both right and left attacks.* This will ensure that the student is capable of defense regardless of the direction of the attack.
- *Low rank students should practice with a large margin for error.* New students should maintain a 12-inch gap between their counter-technique and their target.

This will allow the student to counterattack without fear of injuring their classmates. As the student progresses in rank and their control improves, this gap can be progressively shortened. Appropriate distance is a matter of instructor discretion and will vary based on the student's degree of control, but the following distances may be used as guidelines:

- **White Belt/Yellow Stripe:** 11-12 inches
- **Yellow Belt/Green Stripe:** 9-10 inches
- **Green Belt/Blue Stripe:** 7-8 inches
- **Blue Belt/Brown Stripe:** 5-6 inches
- **Brown Belt/Red Stripe:** 3-4 inches
- **Red Belt/Black Stripe:** 1-2 inches
- **Black Belt:** 0-1 inches (Note: 0 inches means contact without delivery of notable force)

# *Sparring*

Competitive sparring is intended to help develop speed, precision, timing, distance, fluidity, technique and kinesthetic knowledge. Sparring is *not* intended to simulate realistic self-defense; many techniques that will score points and win matches are ill-suited to practical defense on the street (for example, head-high kicks). Similarly, many techniques that are appropriate for legitimate self-defense are not appropriate in most sparring situations (for example, attacking your opponent's knees).

That being said, sparring does have certain practical applications. Proficiency in sparring helps students develop traits that are useful in self-defense, such as accuracy, quick reflexes, timing, balance, an understanding of proper distance and the ability to remain calm under pressure. Sparring should not be mistaken for self-defense, but it should also not be ignored or treated as irrelevant.

The American Kyuki-Do Federation hosts several tournaments each year, to which all AKF members are invited. Interested students should contact their instructor for details.

## Sparring Rules

Specific sparring rules may vary from class to class, but there are some general safety considerations that should be followed:

- During all contact sparring, full sparring gear must be worn. This includes:
    - Head Gear
    - Mouth Guard
    - Foot Pads
    - Hand Pads
    - Shin Guards
    - Groin Cup (for men)
- Legal targets generally include:
    - Midsection (abdomen and chest)
    - Head (light contact with head gear only)
- Non-scoring targets include:
    - Below the Belt
    - Neck
    - Back
    - Shoulders
    - Arms
    - Hands
    - Head (except for light contact to the head gear)
- Deliberate attacks to non-scoring targets will result in warnings, penalties and/or disqualification.
- No grabbing or holding.
- No excessive force (either in striking or blocking).

- Treat your partner, your center judge and your corner judges with respect.
- Safety is your first priority. It is better to lose a match than to run the risk of injuring yourself or your partner.

The AKF always maintains a complete and current set of tournament rules for point sparring, grappling, breaking, forms and weapons competition. Please refer to kyukidomartialarts.com for current rules.

## *Legal Aspects of Self-Defense*

Due to the national and international range of Kyuki-Do and the varying statutes and case law regarding self-defense and the use of force in self-defense, it is highly recommended that practitioners of the art contact their local District Attorney's office or Attorney General's office to become thoroughly familiar with the statutes and case law in their states or countries. In general it is accurate to assume that you are entitled to use as much (but no more) force than is necessary in order to protect yourself or another from injury or death.

Note that in all cases, the best form of self-defense (and the one that is least likely to result in legal issues) is to avoid putting yourself in a situation where it will become necessary to defend yourself. It is the belief of the AKF that in the great majority of situations physical confrontation may be avoided through the use of caution, common sense and conflict resolution.

**CAUTION:** Remember that knowledge of self-defense techniques carries with it the responsibility to use such knowledge only in legitimate self-defense situations, and even then only as a last resort.

# Chapter Five: Weapons Training

Kyuki-Do utilizes weapons that originate from four main areas: Japan, Korea, China and the Philippines. Much of Kyuki-Do's current weapons curriculum is derived from traditional Okinawan Kobudo, which means "Old Warrior Way." In addition to Kobudo, Kyuki-Do utilizes the Japanese Bo staff and Katana or Bokken, as well as the Filipino Kali sticks.

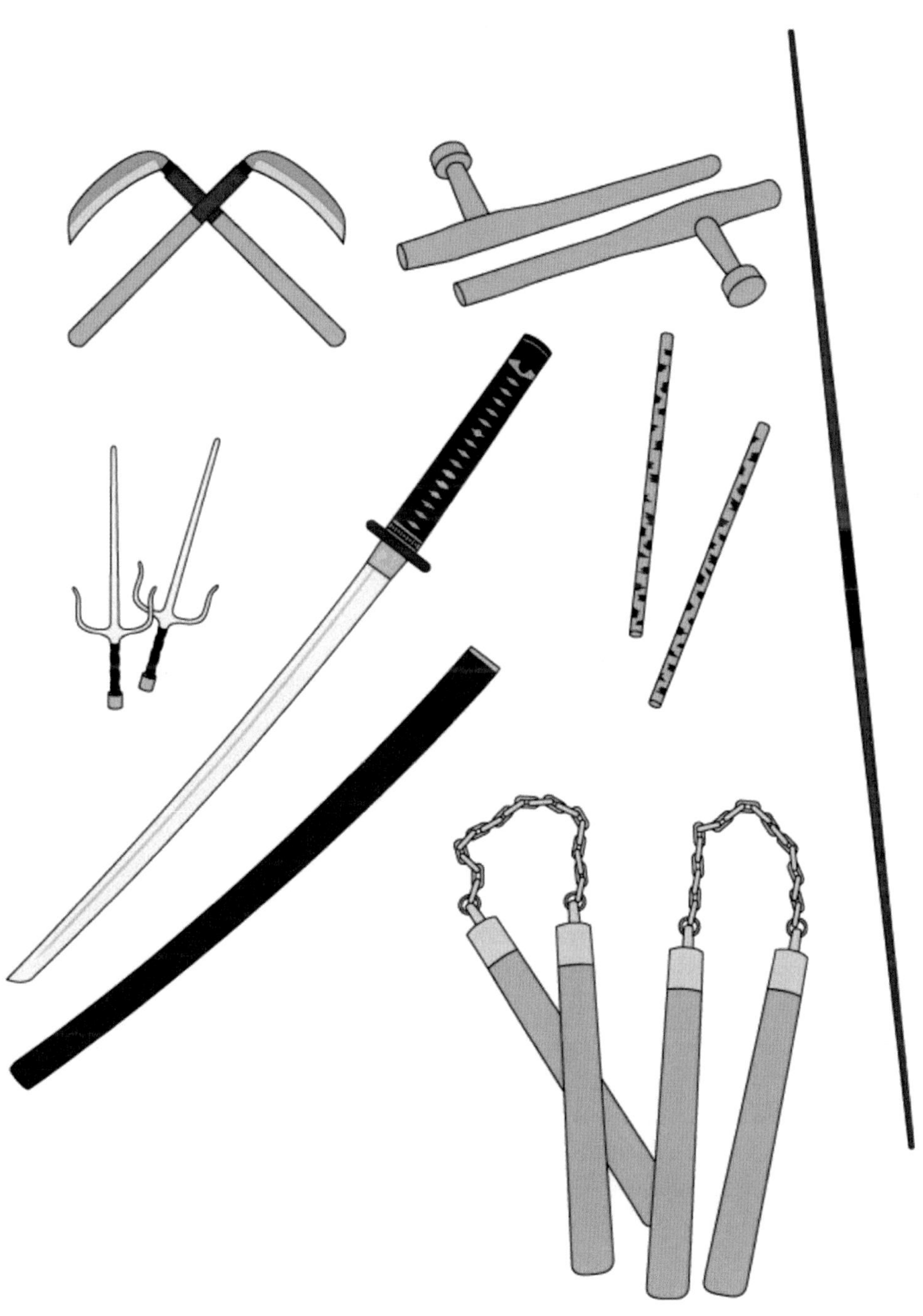

## *Kobudo History and Weapons*

Okinawan Kobudo dates back to the $12^{th}$ century when the Aji (regional lords of Japan) controlled Japan and Okinawa. This was a time of nearly continuous warfare, and many new fighting techniques (both armed and unarmed) were created and perfected during the following several hundred years.

In 1429, Sho Hashi united the island of Japan and founded the Kingdom of the Ryukyus. During the $14^{th}$ to $16^{th}$ centuries (a period known as the "Golden Age of Trade"), the Kingdom of the Ryukyus flourished as a trade center for China, Korea and other nations. However, trade vessels were constantly threatened by Japanese pirates, and the Okinawan sailors needed to protect themselves while in foreign lands.

Around 1850, Toyotomi Hideyoshi set forth laws that prohibited the possession of weapons among the peasantry. This prohibition was intended to prevent loss of life and reduce the possibility of insurrection or civil war. However, it left the peasants of Okinawa more or less defenseless against the Samurai, who were the only ones allowed to carry weapons.

Although the empty-handed techniques developed on the battlefields during earlier centuries were effective and refined, they were ill-suited for large-scale combat and insufficient against the Samurai. In 1609, the Satouma Samurai clan attacked and swept through the Okinawan defenses. The Okinawans fought with simple farming tools, daggers and shields; against well-armed and armored Samurai on horseback, the Okinawans stood little chance.

Out of necessity, the Okinawans developed a martial style that utilized modified farming tools, such as the Nunchaku, Tonfa and Sai, and simple and common weapons like the Bo staff and Jo staff, coupled with the previously developed empty-handed techniques of early Karate. This system eventually came to be known as Okinawan Kobudo.

Various distinct styles of Kobudo emerged during the Ryukyuan Kingdom. These styles were taught in close circles and handed down from master to disciple. In the absence of a strong, centralized Okinawan government, these techniques and styles were never formalized on any sort of national level.

During the Meiji restoration in the $19^{th}$ century the Ryukyuan Kingdom was dissolved. In 1879, Okinawa was annexed by the Japanese government, and the Japanese integrated Karate and Kobudo into the public education system. The early 1900s saw the development of four primary schools of Karate (Shorin-Ryu, Goju-Ryu, Uechi-Ryu and Matsubayashi-Ryu) that integrated the Kobudo system of techniques and weaponry.

## Kobudo Weapons: Nunchaku

The Nunchaku was originally used by the Okinawan farmers to thresh crops such as wheat and rice. The weapon is composed of two pieces of hardwood connected by rope or chain. It is also possible that the original Nunchaku was a horse bridle.

Standard modern Nunchaku are octagonal or round in shape and 12" to 15" in length with a flexible chain or rope of 1" to 4" that connects the two sides and allows the freedom to generate substantial speed and striking power. The customary length of one Nunchaku is the distance from the inside of the elbow to the center of the palm. The connecting chain or rope should measure across the top of the hand so that when draped over the back of the hand the two ends of the weapon hang perpendicular to the floor.

The Nunchaku user can subdue an enemy by using ensnaring actions, traps that either lock or crush, poking, jabbing or sweeping strikes, as well as defensive parrying and deflections. Very effective flailing blows target points like the ribs, clavicles, forearms, wrists, hands, face and knees, while thrusting strikes target points like the throat, groin, eyes and midsection. A painful ensnaring action can be applied by catching the enemy's fingers, hand or wrist in a nutcracker-type grip, forcing them into submission. Using a single Nunchaku with both hands allows the wielder to disguise subsequent striking, kicking or blocking actions, while using two Nunchaku allows the wielder to mount attacks from a greater variety of directions and angles.

While highly effective at close range, the Nunchaku can also keep an opponent at bay from long range as well. The most well-known technique for accomplishing this is the figure eight, which may be performed vertically or horizontally, forward or reverse. A great variety of additional manipulation can be used to switch grips or hands, or to set up for strikes and blocks.

The key to performing an excellent Nunchaku form is to not only focus on the awesome speed and agility that the weapon is known for, but to also demonstrate proper application of power and practical technique. The practice it takes to reach proficiency with the Nunchaku frequently results in a tendency toward the use of excessive manipulation, resulting in a demonstration that is superficially flashy and impressive but fundamentally lacking in realistic application.

Each stick of the Nunchaku is divided into three parts: the upper (jokon-bu), the middle (chukon-bu) and the lower (kibon-bu). The top of the stick is called the knotoh and the hole that the rope passes through is called the ana.

The Korean terminology for the Nunchaku is Sahng Jol Bong.

## Kobudo Weapons: Sai

The Sai is a formidable short, metal, forklike weapon approximately 15" to 20" in length. Disguised as a farming tool that was used to help plant rice seeds, and as a pitchfork during harvest, the Sai has a long history in India, China, Malaysia and Indonesia. The weapon was introduced to Okinawa by the Chinese, and it was quickly found to be very effective as a defensive counter to the katana of the Samurai.

The main shaft of the Sai tapers from a pointed forward end to a blunt, lipped base. The two tines taper to a point and are bent slightly outward. The length of the Sai should be about an inch longer than the wielder's forearm.

Sai are generally used in pairs, but advanced practitioners use three, with one held in the back of the belt ready to be thrown. The proper use of the Sai relies on great manual dexterity and hand strength on the part of the wielder, who will use his or her thumbs as pivot points upon which the center of the weapon is balanced. The tightening and loosening of the grip allow for manipulation of the weapon and consolidation of striking power.

The Korean terminology for the Sai is Jang Tan-Do.

## Kobudo Weapons: Kama

The Kama are short-handled sickles that are usually used in pairs. Kama were originally used to cut down rice stalks at the end of the growing season. Some practitioners tie a loop of rope about four to eight inches long to the end of the handle, which results in a modified version of the Kama knows as the Kusarigama. Other variations include a Kama blade at the end of a Bo staff. As a bladed weapon, much care must be taken when practicing with Kama. Students are encouraged to begin their training with a deliberately dulled practice Kama to lessen the likelihood of injury.

Like Sai, Kama are most effective when wielded as a pair. When fighting, one Kama was typically hidden behind the back, ready for throwing. Kama were efficient and deadly; it is said that even sword masters avoided fighting Kama masters.

The Korean terminology for the Kama is Nat.

## Kobudo Weapons: Tonfa

Many variations of Tonfa exist, but the most common is a short, tapered stick with an off-center handle. The Tonfa were originally used as handles for milling stones (the word Tonfa actually translates as "handle"). The Tonfa are usually used in pairs.

Tonfa may be used for blocks, thrusts and strikes. The wielder may spin the Tonfa around the short handle, thereby generating enormous striking force. The Tonfa may also be used for numerous controlling, locking and pain-compliance techniques, making them an excellent weapon for subduing an opponent without permanent injury. For this reason many police stations have adopted the PR-24 (essentially a modern Tonfa) as a replacement for the less versatile baton.

The Korean terminology for the Tonfa is Cha-Ru.

## *Filipino Kali Sticks*

While sticks are undoubtedly one of the oldest and most basic human weapons (predating even the use of bladed hunting tools), few if any cultures ever developed the art of stick fighting to the degree of sophistication and expertise of Filipino Kali practitioners. Early records of the Malaysian Empire contain references to Kali as the martial art of the Philippines; just as the Okinawan sailors adopted new fighting techniques and weaponry learned from their travels, so too did the Filipino tribes who traveled outside the islands for trade. Numerous outside influences contributed to the development of Kali, including the Arabs, the Indians and the Chinese.

The term Kali refers specifically to the Malay broad-bladed weapon also known as the *kris*, but eventually came to describe the unique blending of Malay, Borneo and native Filipino martial arts. Kali was passed down from the Filipino warriors to the commoners, eventually becoming an art taught nearly universally among the Filipino people.

Kali is an exceptionally effective art, as was demonstrated by the disastrous results of Ferdinand Magellan's initial foray to the Philippines. Magellan, a Portuguese explorer, reached the island of Cebu in the central Philippines on April 7th, 1521. King Humabon and Queen Juana of Cebu were quick to welcome and recognize Magellan as the representative of the King of Spain. However, Rajah Lapulapu of the nearby Mactan Island was not so welcoming; he refused to pay tribute or bow down to the foreigner.

Enraged by this Lapulapu's defiance, Magellan personally led an invasion of Mactan Island. The famous Battle of Mactan took place in the early morning of April 27$^{th}$, 1521.

The Mactan Island warriors, using their traditional fire-hardened rattan sticks, kris swords, lances, poisoned arrows, bolos and sharpened sticks, soundly defeated the well-equipped and professionally trained conquistadors. The bloody battle resulted in Magellan's untimely death and unequivocally demonstrated the power and utility of the humble rattan stick. Eventually the Spanish returned with firearms and conquered the Philippines, maintaining control of the region for almost 400 years.

There are probably over 100 styles of Filipino martial arts, but they can be roughly grouped into three main areas: Northern, Southern and Central. The Northern system became known as Arnis, the Central system as Eskrima or Escrima, and the Southern system (which was characterized by the simultaneous use of two sticks) was Moro.

The Korean terminology for the Kali stick is Than Bong.

## *Bo Staff*

The Bo staff, which has been used throughout human history in some form, consists of a simple wooden pole some 5' to 6' in length. Like many other ancient weapons, the Bo staff doubled as a common tool or farming implement, being used both as a hiking stick and as a method for carrying buckets of water (which were hung from both ends while the Bo itself was slung across the shoulders). The Chinese version of this weapon has non-tapered ends, while the Japanese Bo (sometimes referred to in modern times as a toothpick-style Bo) has gently tapered ends that slightly reduce the weight of the weapon and provide a more concentrated point of impact for jabbing or thrusting strikes.

Bojutsu is a martial system using the Japanese Bo staff. Japanese feudal warriors practiced this art, adapting it from earlier Chinese styles primarily popularized by Daruma Daishi, a Zen priest and leader of the Shorin-ji temple in China around 517 AD. The Katori Shinto-ryu style (founded by Izasha Inenao) is the root from which most of these early systems were derived. Bojutsu was formalized as an art form in Japan around 1192 AD.

The Bo operates best from outside the range of the enemy's weapon, giving the wielder a significant advantage if their opponent is armed with a shorter weapon. Because it is a long-range weapon, the Bo staff works best in relatively open spaces, where the user has the opportunity to utilize the full range of the staff's offensive capabilities. The Bo is still functional at short range, but the wielder then becomes more vulnerable to being cut, caught or struck by the enemy.

Though the Bo is excellent for basic weapons training, mastery does require a lengthy study of fundamental gripping, stances and footwork, as well as the striking, blocking, jabbing and deflecting techniques. The weapon requires a solid base and good stances in order to effectively transfer power, and a proper grip is essential both to master manipulation techniques (generally figure eight spins around the body that are used to act as a shield) and to prevent the enemy from stripping the weapon away. Footwork, stability and clean, level lines to key target areas on the opponent's body are all crucial to attaining excellence with the Bo.

The Korean terminology for the Bo is Jang Bong.

## *Katana*

The Katana is a curved sword with a single edge, designed to be wielded with two hands. Though traditionally thought of as a Japanese weapon, the sword was also an important part of the Korean culture, as evidenced by the Hwarang (Flowering Youth) warriors, a Korean youth group of well-trained nobles that existed during the $6^{th}$ century. In fact, the art of making swords probably came to Japan from China, via Korea. Some of the earliest known examples of sword-making were straight swords called Chokoto that were manufactured in Japan by foreign smiths until about 900 AD.

Kyuki-Do utilizes elements of Iaido, the Way of Drawing the Sword, Kendo, the Way of the Sword, and Haidong Gumdo, a traditional Korean sword style. Iaido and Kendo are Japanese arts that are practiced using Bokken (wooden training swords). High-rank practitioners use Iaito (steel practice swords with a dulled edge) or Shinken Katanas (live steel). Iaido practice includes drawing the sword, defensive and cutting motions and replacement of the sword in its scabbard. The motions are intended to simulate defense against an attack by an imaginary opponent.

Iaido may seem odd or limited to those who do not have a clear understanding of the history of the art. The emphasis on drawing the sword dates back to the days when these techniques were actually used in armed combat. A fraction of a second of time or a millimeter of distance could make all the difference in the outcome of a match between swordsmen. Since the swords were razor-sharp, even a relatively minor cut could mean death, so getting the sword out of the scabbard and into proper position was crucial.

Of course, what we practice now is an art form, with the focus on correct form, efficient motion and proper technique rather than the actual application of a killing blow. By continually refining our technique with the sword we can improve our concentration and focus as well as strengthen our bodies.

The Korean terminology for the Katana is Kum.

## *Weapons Form Criteria*

Advanced colored belt students will be expected to develop a personal weapons form prior to their promotion to black belt. The following are general points to consider when creating and demonstrating such a form.

1) **Presentation:** Before beginning the form the student should present to the judges or testing board. Proper presentation includes stating one's name and school and the name of the form.
2) **Break In and Break Out:** The Break In and Break Out (sometimes called the Bow In and Bow Out) is a brief series of movements performed at the beginning and end of the form, generally intended to demonstrate the student's power and control as well as serving as a marker for the beginning and ending of the form. The Break In and Break Out are considered optional.
3) **Weapon Control:** The student must demonstrate excellent control of the weapon and comfort with its use. The concept of Sword of No Sword indicates a state wherein the student has attained such a high degree of proficiency with their weapon that it is treated as though it were an extension of their own body. This level of control should ideally be demonstrated during any weapons form. Note: loss of control of one's weapon is generally grounds for disqualification when competing with a weapon form.
4) **Basic Technique:** All weapon forms should display fundamental techniques such as stances, blocks, strikes and kicks.
5) **Body Conditioning:** Body conditioning refers to the act of striking one's body with the weapon in order to either toughen the body and/or change the direction of the weapon. Note that body conditioning is only applicable when using non-bladed weapons.
6) **Application to Self-Defense:** All elements of a weapons form should be realistic and applicable. The student should have a clear understanding of what each move is intended to represent and how it would function in practical application.
7) **Classical Pose:** Classical poses are traditional, exaggerated poses that are intended to demonstrate balance and flexibility as well as to showcase the beauty of the weapon itself.
8) **Theory:** Theory refers to a specific, logical sequence of moves with a weapon. Each weapon has a different sequence, and some forms may have multiple possible sequences.
9) **Weapon Manipulation:** Manipulation (rolling, spinning or flipping the weapon) demonstrates the student's mastery and control, highlights the beauty of proper usage and, in a practical sense, serves to intimidate or disorient an opponent. When developing a weapon form it is important to remember that manipulation should make up only a small portion of the form and it should never replace basic technique or practical application.
10) **Composition:** Composition indicates that a form follows a pattern that is aesthetically pleasing and that the student demonstrates an overall competence and high standard of performance.

# Chapter Six: Kyuki-Do and Its Forms

As in most martial arts, Kyuki-Do teaches its students certain forms or hyungs. These forms vary in length and complexity. The main purpose of these forms is to sharpen the individual's concentration and engage the mind totally in the execution and perfection of certain movements. Mastery of these forms is achieved when one is able to unite one's body and mind in the performance of these forms. As the forms become progressively more difficult, the student is challenged by each subsequent form to develop even greater powers of cocentration.

In addition to helping the student develop proper concentration, the forms establish fighting strategies or skills through which the student practices various stances, blocks, punches and kicks. They are an excellent way of developing strength, speed, technical precision and balance.

The forms are also used as a measuring scale of one's devotion and commitment to the basic teachings of Kyuki-Do. They are a required element for belt promotion, so one is required to study and master a number of forms as one continues to learn and develop in Kyuki-Do.

Dedicated and regular practice of the forms will help the student do the following:

- Develop better sparring techniques
- Improve flexiblity
- Control body movement
- Build muscle
- Develop proper breathing patterns
- Develop smooth and rhythmical movement
- Develop an internal sense of direction, equilibrium and kinesthetic awareness
- Develop speed and focus
- Focus the mind and improve concentration
- Apply the Theory of Power

The forms of Kyuki-Do were specifically designed by the Masters of the AKF to unite the Federation and to separate Kyuki-Do from other martial arts. For this reason, Kyuki-Do's forms incorporate a variety of different techniques including falls, throws, chokes, joint locks, take-downs and weapons, as well as the kicks, strikes and blocks that form the mainstay of so many other arts' forms.

## *The Meaning Behind the Forms*

Practicing the forms of Kyuki-Do challenges the mind of the student in another way that goes beyond the simple memorization of physical movements; each form has its own meaning that the student is expected to learn and memorize.

The most important element of Kyuki-Do's forms is the meaning that underlies the pattern. These meanings illustrate and highlight important life concepts that the student is expected to understand. The meanings of the forms are intended to clarify the student's philosophical and moral obligations to themselves, to other people and to society as a whole.

In addition to the meaning assigned to each form, which you will find on each form's opening page in the sections that follow, there is significance attached to the chun-bi position and to the number of movements as well. Each form has a number of movements that is representative of a unit of time:

- Kibon—the twelve movements represent the twelve months in a year.
- Kicho—the twenty-four movements represent the twenty-four hours in a day.
- Kyuki Il Chang—the thirty movements represent the days of some months. The chun-bi position represents strength (the closed fist) and control (the open hand covering the fist).
- Kyuki Yee Chang—the thirty-one movements represent the days of some months. The chun-bi position represents strength (the closed fist) and control (the open hand covering the fist).
- Kyuki Sam Chang—the twenty-nine movements represent the twenty-nine days in February in a leap year. The chun-bi position represents strength (the closed fist) and control (the open hand covering the fist).
- Gucn Bon—the twenty-eight movements represent the twenty-eight days in February in a non-leap year. The chun-bi position represents planting a tree.
- Chon Ji In Il Chang—the thirty-three movements represent infinity: heaven, earth and people and mind, body and spirit. The chun-bi position represents the sky.
- Chon Ji In Yee Chang—the thirty-three movements represent infinity: heaven, earth and people and mind, body and spirit. The chun-bi position represents the earth.
- Chon Ji In Sam Chang—the thirty-three movements represent infinity: heaven, earth and people and mind, body and spirit. The chun-bi position represents people.
- Man Nam—the fifty-two movements represent the fifty-two weeks in a year.
- Ka Chi—the thirty-six movements represent the minimum number of months that a dedicated student will take to travel the path from white belt to black belt. The chun-bi position represents two people walking side by side.
- Sa Rang—the thirty-three movements represent infinity: heaven, earth and people and mind, body and spirit. The chun-bi position represents love.
- Kyuki-Do Nakbop Hyung—the twelve movements represent the twelve months in a year.

## *The Belt Ranking System and the Meaning of the Belt Colors*

Like many other martial arts, Kyuki-Do incorporates a ranking system that utilizes colored belts. The color of a student's belt symbolizes his or her progression in the art; students start at white belt, and as they become more and more proficient, they promote to higher ranks. Kyuki-Do has twelve colored belt ranks before black belt. There are six solid belt colors and six stripe ranks. The colors are based on the life cycle of a tree as it goes through the four seasons of the year. Each rank has a month associated with it.

The new student starts out as a white belt. The white belt represents a seed underneath the winter snow. Just as the seed has the potential to develop and grow into a healthy tree the new student has the potential for spiritual, mental and physical growth. The month associated with a white belt is January.

The next belt color is yellow. The yellow belt represents the sun. It's the sun that melts the snow causing the seed to germinate. February is the month represented by the yellow stripe belt (a white belt with a yellow stripe around it), and the solid yellow belt represents March.

Green is the color of spring. In springtime growth and activity abound. Just like the lush and vibrant young sapling, the student experiences significant growth at this rank. April is represented by the green stripe while a green belt represents May.

After green comes blue. The blue belt represents the summer sky. Like a tree growing toward the sky, the students strive to reach their full potential. The blue stripe belt represents the month of June and the solid blue belt represents July.

Brown represents maturity. The brown belt represents the bark of the mature tree, as well as the way that other plants turn to brown in the later part of summer. The brown belt student has started to develop and mature into a serious martial artist. August is the month represented by brown stripe. A brown belt represents the month of September.

Red is the last color before black. Just as the leaves turning red in the fall warn us to be prepared for the coming of winter, the red belt warns the student that they are coming to the end of their first cycle and to prepare for the start of their next cycle, which begins with a 1$^{st}$ degree black belt. The red stripe represents October, a solid red belt represents November and a black stripe represents the month of December.

The black belt is the color of knowledge and proficiency. The black belt represents the completion of an earlier cycle (kup ranks; colored belts), which now starts again from the beginning (dan ranks; black belt levels).

**The Belt Ranking System of Kyuki-Do:**

| **Type of Belt** | **Rank** | **Month/Season** |
|---|---|---|
| Junior White Belt | $12^{th}$ Kup | January (Winter) |
| Senior White Belt (Yellow Stripe) | $11^{th}$ Kup | February (Winter) |
| Junior Yellow Belt | $10^{th}$ Kup | March (Winter) |
| Senior Yellow Belt (Green Stripe) | $9^{th}$ Kup | April (Spring) |
| Junior Green Belt | $8^{th}$ Kup | May (Spring) |
| Senior Green Belt (Blue Stripe) | $7^{th}$ Kup | June (Spring) |
| Junior Blue Belt | $6^{th}$ Kup | July (Summer) |
| Senior Blue Belt (Brown Stripe) | $5^{th}$ Kup | August (Summer) |
| Junior Brown Belt | $4^{th}$ Kup | September (Summer) |
| Senior Brown Belt (Red Stripe) | $3^{rd}$ Kup | October (Fall) |
| Junior Red Belt | $2^{nd}$ Kup | November (Fall) |
| Senior Red Belt (Black Stripe) | $1^{st}$ Kup | December (Fall) |

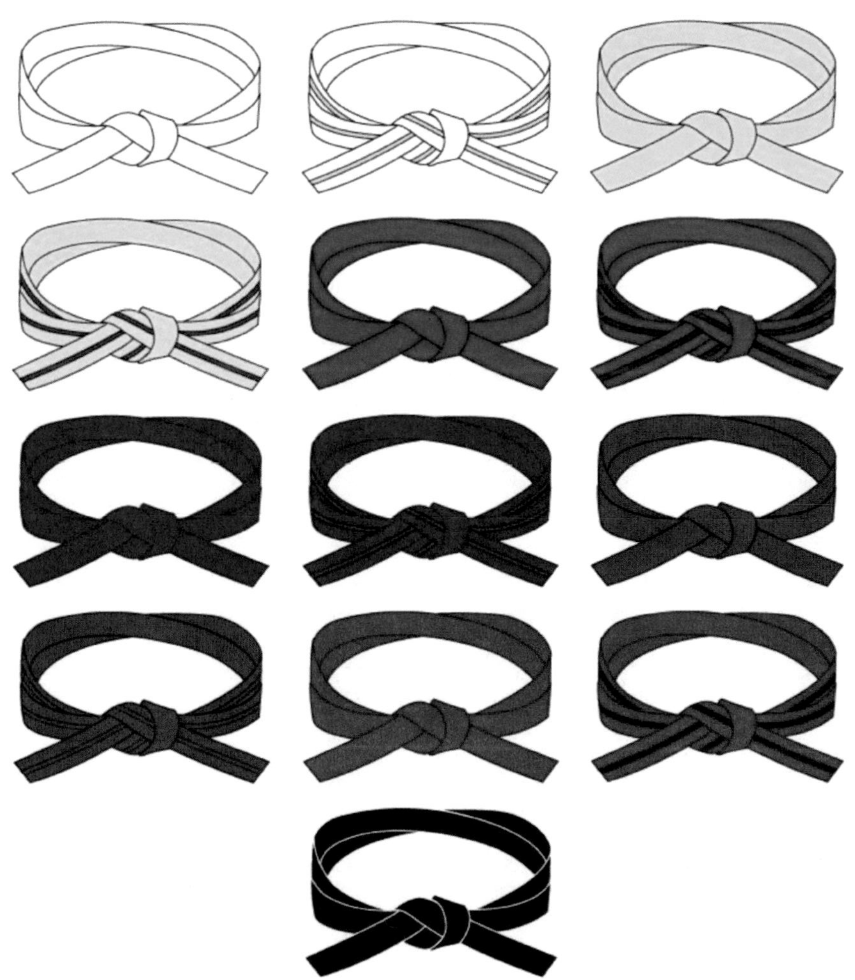

## *The Forms of Kyuki-Do*

The following section of the handbook provides a step-by-step walkthrough of each of Kyuki-Do's yukupja (colored belt) forms. Each form is illustrated with photographs of one of the AKF Masters executing the form and includes proper Korean terminology for each technique. Steps that include kihaps are written in red.

Forms should only be learned under the supervision of a qualified instructor! The walkthroughs included in this handbook are intended to serve as a supplement to the student's training; attempting to learn the forms from this book without proper supervision is likely to result in flawed technique.

Further information on the forms (including detailed walkthroughs from multiple angles, as well as examples of the practical application of the movements in the forms) is provided to active AKF members on kyukidomartialarts.com.

# 기본

# Kibon

(12 Movements)
Presented by Grand Master Ken Ok Hyung Kim

**Kibon:** **Basic** or **Beginning.**
Principle building blocks for your training, both mental and physical.

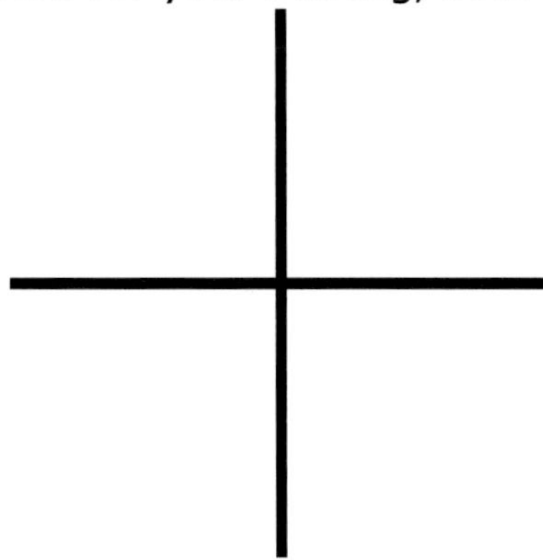

**Ready Position:**
Parallel Stance.

1: Begin by turning left 90 degrees toward **B**, forming a **left foot forward front stance** (wen bal ahp sogi) while executing a left **high section forearm block** (sahngdan palmok makgi). **Kihap**.

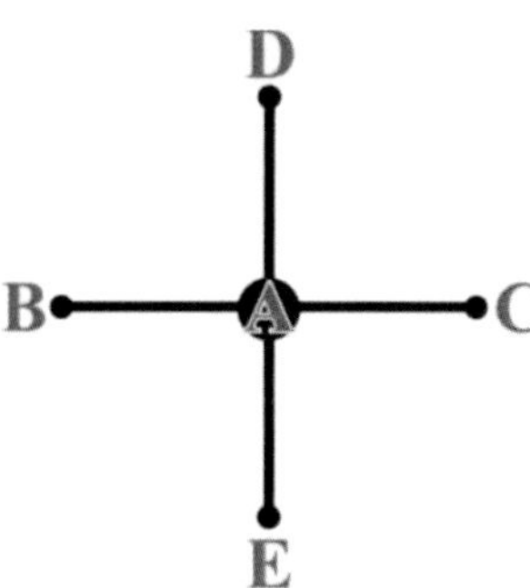

2: Step forward with right foot toward **B**, forming a **right foot forward front stance** (orun bal ahp sogi) while executing a right **high section front punch** (sahngdan ahp joomok chirugi).

3: Turn to your right 180 degrees toward **C**, forming a **right foot forward front stance** (orun bal ahp sogi) while executing a right **high section forearm block** (sahngdan palmok makgi).

4: Step forward with left foot toward **C**, forming a **left foot forward front stance** (wen bal ahp sogi) while executing a left **high section front punch** (sahngdan ahp joomok chirugi).

5: Turn to your left 90 degrees toward **D**, forming a **left foot forward front stance** (wen bal ahp sogi) while executing a left **high section forearm block** (sahngdan palmok makgi).

6: Step forward with your right foot toward **D**, forming a **right foot forward front stance** (orun bal ahp sogi) while executing a right **high section front punch** (sahngdan ahp joomok chirugi).

7: Turn to your right 180 degrees toward **E**, forming a **right foot forward front stance** (orun bal ahp sogi) while executing a right **high section forearm block** (sahngdan palmok makgi).

7, Alternate View

8: Step forward with left foot toward **E**, forming a **left foot forward front stance** (wen bal ahp sogi) while executing a left **high section front punch** (sahngdan ahp joomok chirugi).

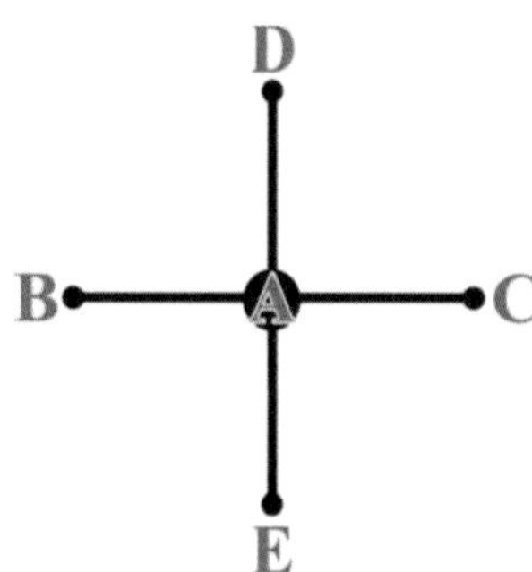

8, Alternate View

9: Turn to your right 180 degrees toward **D**, forming a **right foot forward front stance** (orun bal ahp sogi) while executing a right **high section forearm block** (sahngdan palmok makgi).

9, Continued

10: Move forward toward **D** by executing a left leg **front snap kick** (ahp chagi) and landing in a **left foot forward front stance** (wen bal ahp sogi). Maintain hand positions during kick.

10, Continued

11: Without stepping forward, execute a left **high section front punch** (sahngdan ahp joomok chirugi) toward **D**.

12: Without stepping forward, execute a right **reverse high section punch** (sahngdan bahndae ahp joomok chirugi). **Kihap**.

***Paro:*** Return Left Leg to Ready Position.

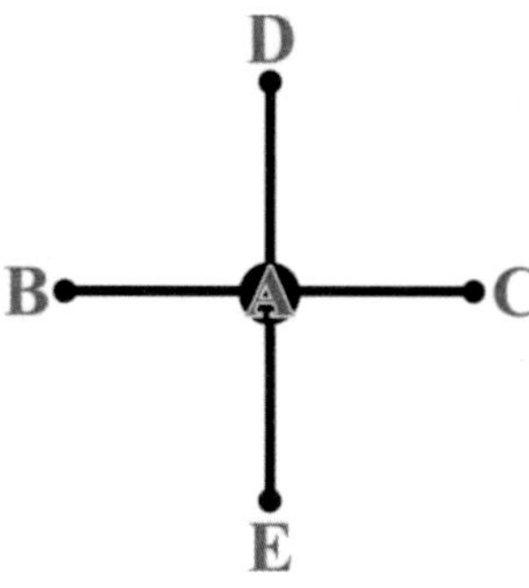

Students testing for yellow stripe must know form Kibon.

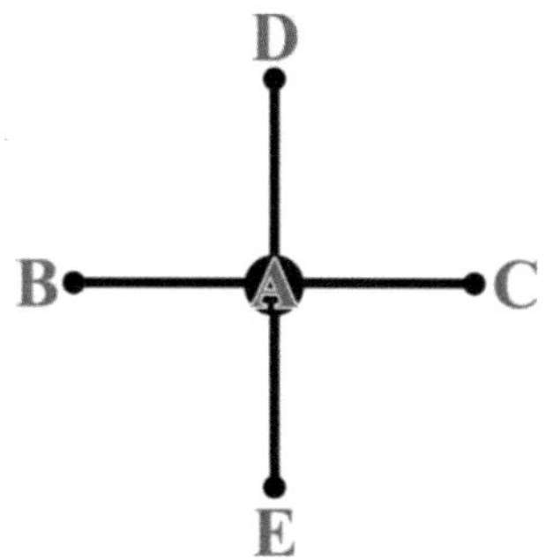


**Kibon: Basic or Beginning.** Principle building blocks for your training, both mental and physical.

**Ready Position:** Parallel stance at A facing D.

**Movements:**

1: Begin by turning left 90 degrees toward **B**, forming a **left foot forward front stance** (wen bal ahp sogi) while executing a left **high section forearm block** (sahngdan palmok makgi). **Kihap**.

2: Step forward with right foot toward **B**, forming a **right foot forward front stance** (orun bal ahp sogi) while executing a right **high section front punch** (sahngdan ahp joomok chirugi).

3: Turn to your right 180 degrees toward **C**, forming a **right foot forward front stance** (orun bal ahp sogi) while executing a right **high section forearm block** (sahngdan palmok makgi).

4: Step forward with left foot toward **C**, forming a **left foot forward front stance** (wen bal ahp sogi) while executing a left **high section front punch** (sahngdan ahp joomok chirugi).

5: Turn to your left 90 degrees toward **D**, forming a **left foot forward front stance** (wen bal ahp sogi) while executing a left **high section forearm block** (sahngdan palmok makgi).

6: Step forward with your right foot toward **D**, forming a **right foot forward front stance** (orun bal ahp sogi) while executing a right **high section front punch** (sahngdan ahp joomok chirugi).

7: Turn to your right 180 degrees toward **E**, forming a **right foot forward front stance** (orun bal ahp sogi) while executing a right **high section forearm block** (sahngdan palmok makgi).

8: Step forward with left foot toward **E**, forming a **left foot forward front stance** (wen bal ahp sogi) while executing a left **high section front punch** (sahngdan ahp joomok chirugi).

9: Turn to your right 180 degrees toward **D**, forming a **right foot forward front stance** (orun bal ahp sogi) while executing a right **high section forearm block** (sahngdan palmok makgi).

10: Move forward toward **D** by executing a left leg **front snap kick** (ahp chagi) and landing in a **left foot forward front stance** (wen bal ahp sogi). Maintain hand positions during kick.

11: Without stepping forward, execute a left **high section front punch** (sahngdan ahp joomok chirugi) toward **D**.

12: Without stepping forward, execute a right **reverse high section punch** (sahngdan bahndae ahp joomok chirugi). **Kihap**.

***Paro:*** Return Left Leg to Ready Position.

# 기초

# Kicho

(24 Movements)
Presented by Grand Master Yun Kim

**Kicho:** **Foundation.** A solid foundation on which to build and develop your martial arts potential.

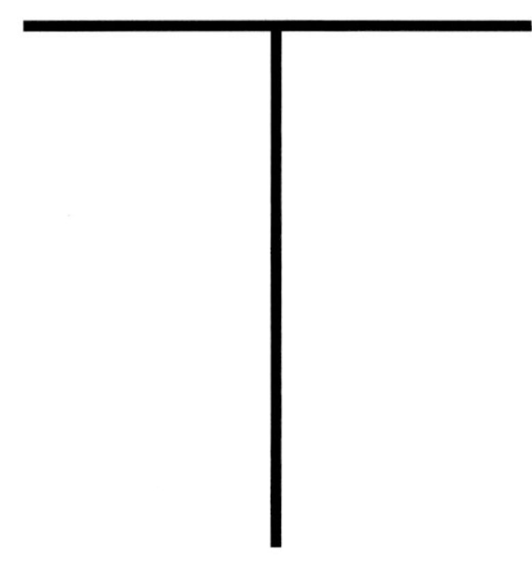

**Ready Position:**
Parallel Stance.

1: Begin by stepping toward **B**, forming a **left foot forward front stance** (wen bal ahp sogi) while executing a left **low section forearm block** (hadan palmok makgi). **Kihap**.

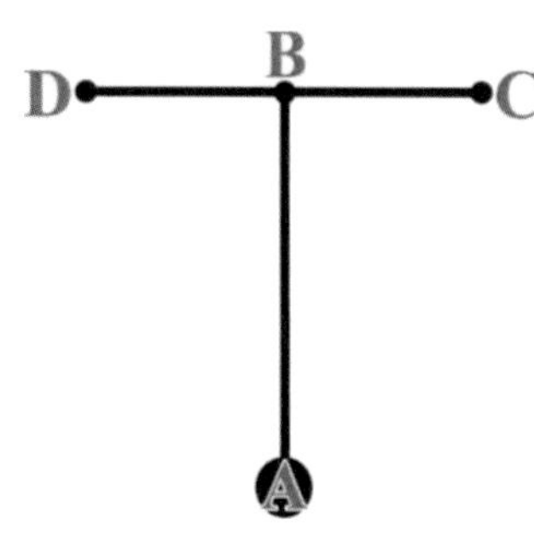

2: Maintain stance. Execute a left **middle section forearm block** (chungdan palmok makgi).

3: Move forward toward **B** by executing a right leg **front snap kick** (ahp chagi) and landing in a **right foot forward front stance** (orun bal ahp sogi).

3, Continued

4: Without stepping forward, execute a right **middle section front punch** (chungdan ahp joomok chirugi) toward **B**.

5: Move forward toward **B** by executing a left leg **front snap kick** (ahp chagi) and landing in a **left foot forward front stance** (wen bal ahp sogi).

5, Continued

6: Without stepping forward, execute a left **middle section front punch** (chungdan ahp joomok chirugi) toward **B**.

7: Step forward with right foot toward **B**, forming a **right foot forward front stance** (orun bal ahp sogi) while executing a right **middle section front punch** (chungdan ahp joomok chirugi).

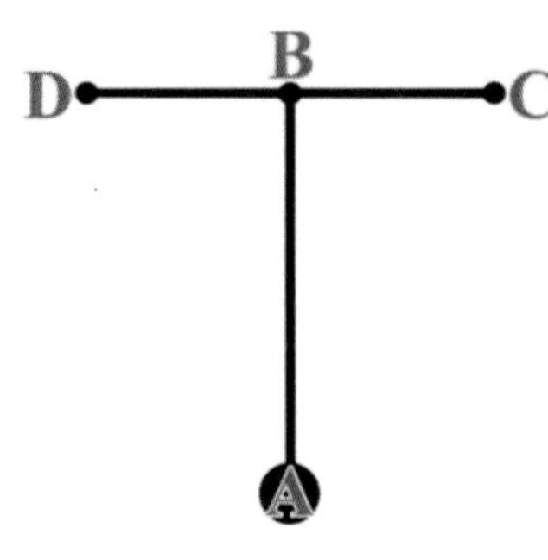

8: Without stepping forward, execute a left **reverse middle section front punch** (chungdan bahndae ahp joomok chirugi) toward **B**. **Kihap.**

9: Turn to your left (counterclockwise) 270 degrees toward **C** (move your left foot). Step into a **left foot forward back stance** (wen bal dwi sogi) while executing left **middle section inside forearm block** (chungdan ahn palmok makgi).

10: Shift left leg into **left foot forward front stance** (wen bal ahp sogi) while executing left **low section forearm block** (hadan palmok makgi).

11: Maintain stance while executing a left **middle section forearm block** (chungdan palmok makgi).

12: Move forward toward **C** by executing a right leg **front snap kick** (ahp chagi) and landing in a **right foot forward front stance** (orun bal ahp sogi).

12, Continued

13: Without stepping forward, execute a right **middle section front punch** (chungdan ahp joomok chirugi) toward **C**

14: Turn to your right (clockwise) 180 degrees toward **D** (move your right foot). Step into a **right foot forward back stance** (orun bal dwi sogi) while executing right **middle section inside forearm block** (chungdan ahn palmok makgi).

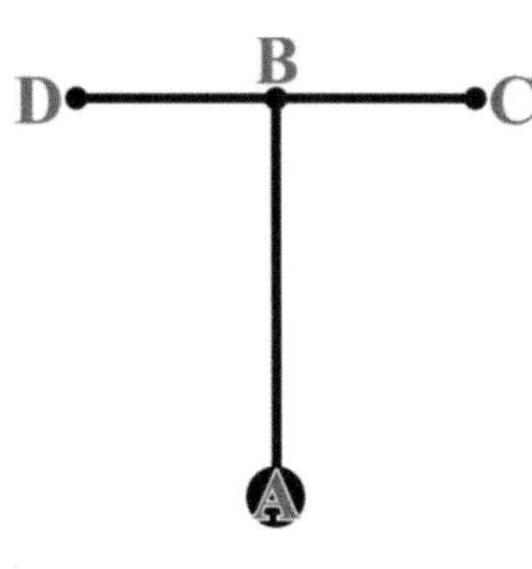

15: Shift right leg into **right foot forward front stance** (orun bal ahp sogi) while executing right **low section forearm block** (hadan palmok makgi).

16: Maintain stance while executing a right **middle section forearm block** (chungdan palmok makgi).

17: Move forward toward **D** by executing a left leg **front snap kick** (ahp chagi) and landing in a **left foot forward front stance** (wen bal ahp sogi).

17, Continued

18: Without stepping forward, execute a left **middle section front punch** (chungdan ahp joomok chirugi) toward **D**.

19: Turn to your left (counterclockwise) 90 degrees toward **A** (move your left foot). Step into a **left foot forward front stance** (wen bal ahp sogi), executing a left **low section forearm block** (hadan palmok makgi).

19, continued

20: Shift your right foot to your left foot, forming a transitional **closed stance** (moa sogi). Step out with your left foot toward **A**, landing in a **left foot forward front stance** (wen bal ahp sogi), executing a left **middle section forearm block** (chungdan palmok makgi).

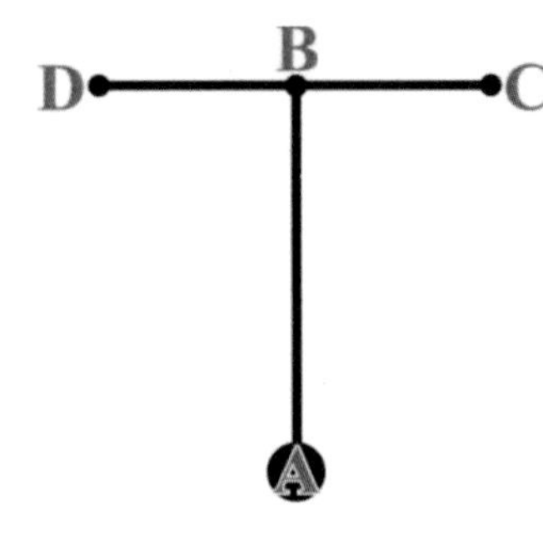


20, Alternate View

20, Continued

20, Alternate View

21: Step forward toward **A** into a **right foot forward front stance** (orun bal ahp sogi), executing a right **middle section front punch** (chungdan ahp joomok chirugi).

21, Alternate View

22: Step forward toward **A** into a **left foot forward front stance** (wen bal ahp sogi), executing a left **middle section front punch** (chungdan ahp joomok chirugi).

22, Alternate View

23: Step forward toward **A** into a **right foot forward front stance** (orun bal ahp sogi), executing a right **middle section front punch** (chungdan ahp joomok chirugi).

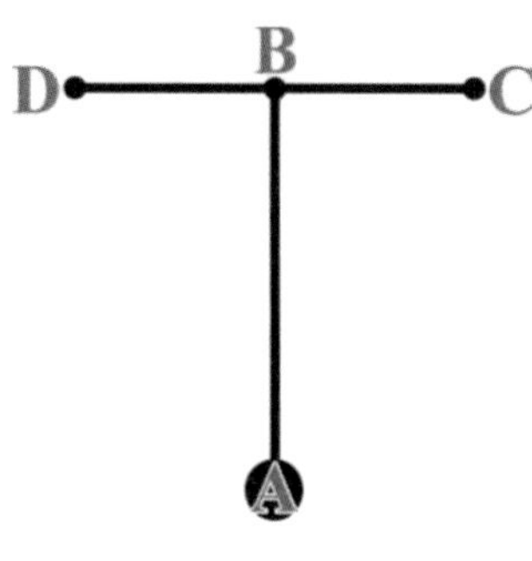

23, Alternate View

24: Maintain stance and execute a left **reverse middle section front punch** (chungdan bahndae ahp joomok chirugi). **Kihap.**

24, Alternate View

***Paro:*** Return Turning Left Leg Counterclockwise to Ready Position.

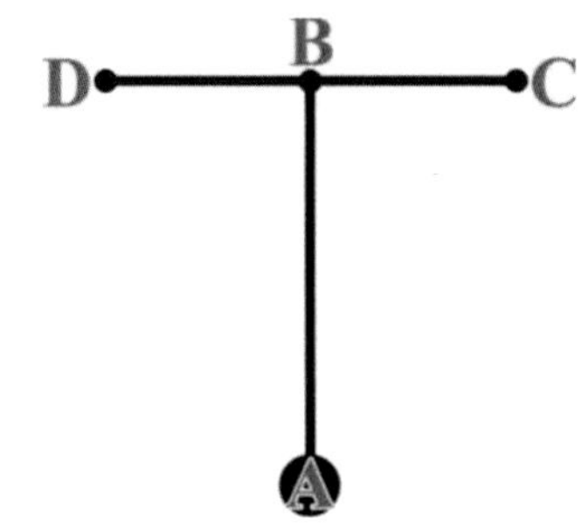

Students testing for yellow belt must know form Kicho.

**Kicho: Foundation.** A solid foundation on which to build and develop your martial arts potential.
**Ready Position:** Parallel stance at A facing D.
**Movements:**

1: Begin by stepping toward **B**, forming a **left foot forward front stance** (wen bal ahp sogi) while executing a left **low section forearm block** (hadan palmok makgi). **Kihap**.

2: Maintain stance. Execute a left **middle section forearm block** (chungdan palmok makgi).

3: Move forward toward **B** by executing a right leg **front snap kick** (ahp chagi) and landing in a **right foot forward front stance** (orun bal ahp sogi).

4: Without stepping forward, execute a right **middle section front punch** (chungdan ahp joomok chirugi) toward **B**.

5: Move forward toward **B** by executing a left leg **front snap kick** (ahp chagi) and landing in a **left foot forward front stance** (wen bal ahp sogi).

6: Without stepping forward, execute a left **middle section front punch** (chungdan ahp joomok chirugi) toward **B**.

7: Step forward with right foot toward **B**, forming a **right foot forward front stance** (orun bal ahp sogi) while executing a right **middle section front punch** (chungdan ahp joomok chirugi).

8: Without stepping forward, execute a left **reverse middle section front punch** (chungdan bahndae ahp joomok chirugi) toward **B**. **Kihap.**

9: Turn to your left (counterclockwise) 270 degrees toward **C** (move your left foot). Step into a **left foot forward back stance** (wen bal dwi sogi) while executing left **middle section inside forearm block** (chungdan ahn palmok makgi).

10: Shift left leg into **left foot forward front stance** (wen bal ahp sogi) while executing left **low section forearm block** (hadan palmok makgi).

11: Maintain stance while executing a left **middle section forearm block** (chungdan palmok makgi).

12: Move forward toward **C** by executing a right leg **front snap kick** (ahp chagi) and landing in a **right foot forward front stance** (orun bal ahp sogi).

13: Without stepping forward, execute a right **middle section front punch** (chungdan ahp joomok chirugi) toward **C**.

14: Turn to your right (clockwise) 180 degrees toward **D** (move your right foot). Step into a **right foot forward back stance** (orun bal dwi sogi) while executing right **middle section inside forearm block** (chungdan ahn palmok makgi).

15: Shift right leg into **right foot forward front stance** (orun bal ahp sogi) while executing right **low section forearm block** (hadan palmok makgi).

16: Maintain stance while executing a right **middle section forearm block** (chungdan palmok makgi).

17: Move forward toward **D** by executing a left leg **front snap kick** (ahp chagi) and landing in a **left foot forward front stance** (wen bal ahp sogi).

18: Without stepping forward, execute a left **middle section front punch** (chungdan ahp joomok chirugi) toward **D**.

19: Turn to your left (counterclockwise) 90 degrees toward **A** (move your left foot). Step into a **left foot forward front stance** (wen bal ahp sogi), executing a left **low section forearm block** (hadan palmok makgi).

20: Shift your right foot to your left foot, forming a transitional **closed stance** (moa sogi). Step out with your left foot toward **A**, landing in a **left foot forward front stance** (wen bal ahp sogi), executing a left **middle section forearm block** (chungdan palmok makgi).

21: Step forward toward **A** into a **right foot forward front stance** (orun bal ahp sogi), executing a right **middle section front punch** (chungdan ahp joomok chirugi).

22: Step forward toward **A** into a **left foot forward front stance** (wen bal ahp sogi), executing a left **middle section front punch** (chungdan ahp joomok chirugi).

23: Step forward toward **A** into a **right foot forward front stance** (orun bal ahp sogi), executing a right **middle section front punch** (chungdan ahp joomok chirugi).

24: Maintain stance and execute a left **reverse middle section front punch** (chungdan bahndae ahp joomok chirugi). **Kihap.**

***Paro:*** Return Turning Left Leg Counterclockwise to Ready Position.

# 격기일장

# Kyuki Il Chang

(30 Movements)
Presented by Grand Master Lloyd Holden

**Kyuki Il Chang:** **Spark Spirit.** Kyuki-Do's ability to awaken the spiritual potential within each of us.

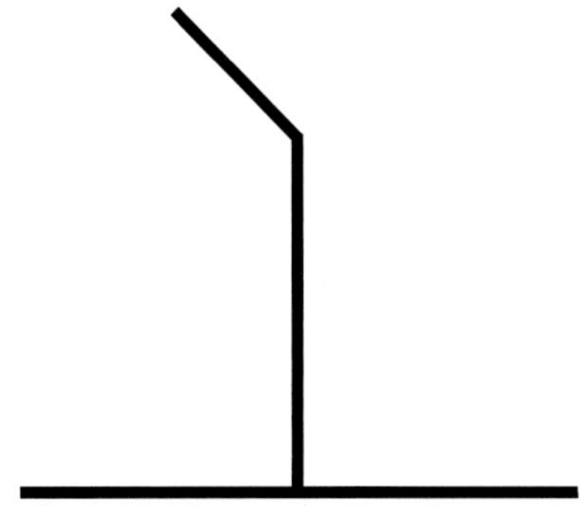

**Ready Position:** Closed Stance AKF Hand Position.

1: Begin by stepping toward **B**, forming a **left foot forward back stance** (wen bal dwi sogi) while executing a left **middle section double knifehand block** (chungdan dool sohn-kal makgi). **Kihap**.

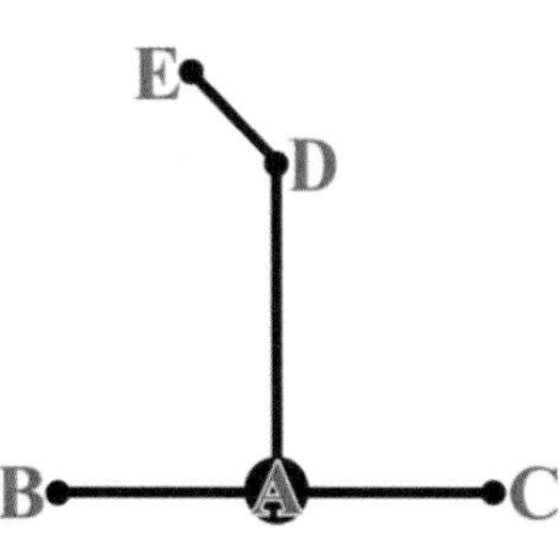

2: Shift left foot toward **B**, forming **left foot forward front stance** (wen bal ahp sogi) while executing a right **reverse middle section knifehand block** (chungdan bahndae sohn-kal makgi).

2, Continued

3: Hook right hand and step with left foot onto line **AB** into a **horse stance** (kima sogi). Execute a left **outside forearm strike** (pakat palmok darigi) to the elbow.

3, Continued

4: Shift left foot to right into a transitional **closed stance** (moa sogi). Step out with right foot into a **right foot forward back stance** (orun bal dwi sogi) while executing a right **middle section double knifehand block** (chungdan dool sohn-kal makgi).

4, Continued

5: Shift right foot toward **C**, forming **right foot forward front stance** (orun bal ahp sogi) while executing a left **reverse middle section knifehand block** (chungdan bahndae sohn-kal makgi).

5, Continued

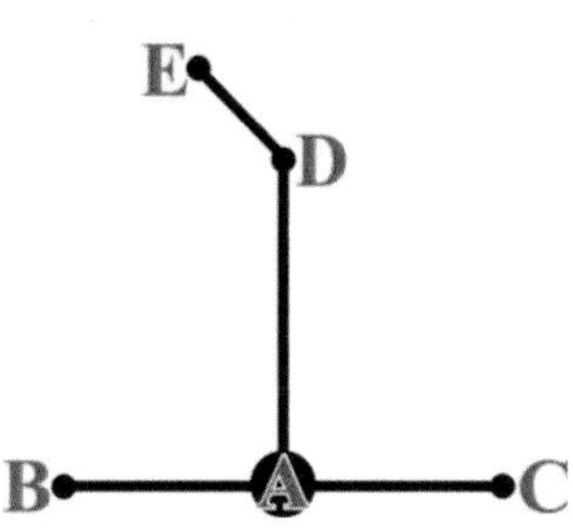

6: Hook left hand and step with right foot onto line **AC** into a **horse stance** (kima sogi). Execute a right **outside forearm strike** (pakat palmok darigi) to the elbow.

6, Continued

7: Shift right foot to left foot into a transitional **closed stance** (moa sogi). Step out with left foot toward **D**, forming a **left foot forward back stance** (wen bal dwi sogi) while executing a left **middle section double knifehand block** (chungdan dool sohn-kal makgi).

7, Continued

8: Shift left foot toward **D**, forming a **left foot forward front stance** (wen bal ahp sogi). Reach out with left hand and grab opponent's head. Execute a right **reverse high section front elbow strike** (sahngdan bahndae ahp palkumchi darigi) with your right elbow coming to meet your left hand.

8, Continued

9: Step forward with your right foot into a **right foot forward back stance** (orun bal dwi sogi) while executing a right **middle section double knifehand block** (chungdan dool sohn-kal makgi).

9, Continued

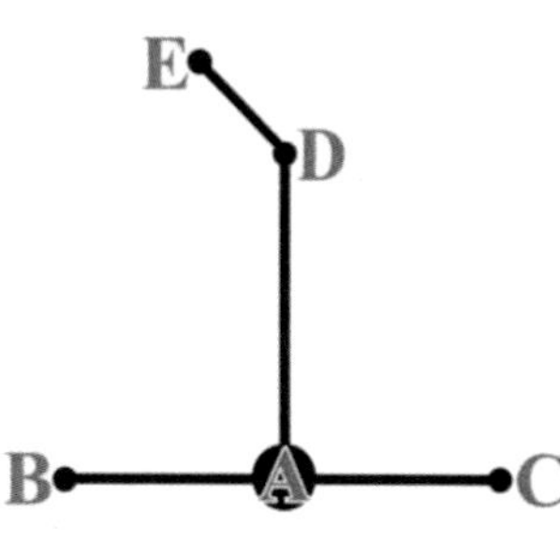

10: Shift right foot toward **D**, forming a **right foot forward front stance** (orun bal ahp sogi). Reach out with right hand and grab opponent's head. Execute a left **reverse high section front elbow strike** (sahngdan bahndae ahp palkumchi darigi) with your left elbow coming to meet your right hand.

10, Continued

11: Step forward toward **D**, forming a **left foot forward front stance** (wen bal ahp sogi). Execute a left **middle section front punch** (chungdan ahp joomok chirugi).

12: Maintain stance. Execute a right **reverse middle section front punch** (chungdan bahndae ahp joomok chirugi). **Kihap.**

13: Look to your left at a 45-degree angle toward **E**, and bring your hands up to a **guarding position** (daebi makgi). Execute a **roundhouse kick** (tollyo chagi) with your right leg. Land in a **right foot forward front stance** (orun bal ahp sogi) facing **E**. Immediately execute number 14.

13, Continued

14: Maintain stance and execute a right **middle section knifehand block** (chungdan sohn-kal makgi).

14, Continued

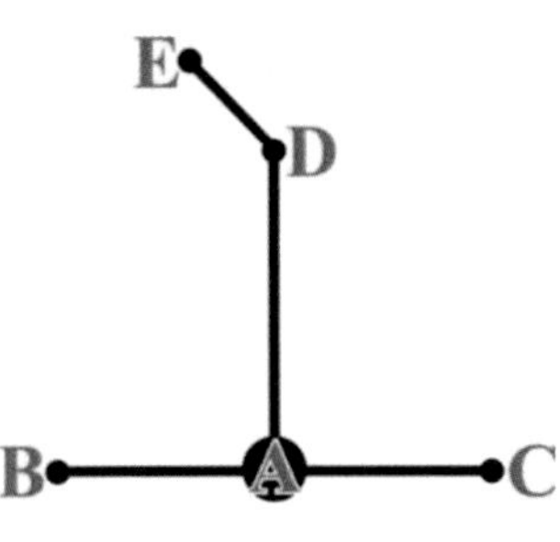

15: Maintain stance and execute a left **reverse high section palm heel strike** (sahngdan bahndae sohn-bahdahk chirugi).

16: Maintain stance and execute a right **high section palm heel strike** (sahngdan sohn-bahdahk chirugi). **Kihap.**

17: Stepping backwards toward **A**, bring right foot to left foot forming a transitional **closed stance** (moa sogi). Step back with left foot into a **right foot forward back stance** (orun bal dwi sogi) executing a right **lower section double knifehand block** (hadan dool sohn-kal makgi).

17, Continued

18: Shift out with the right foot into a **right foot forward front stance** (orun bal ahp sogi) and execute a left **reverse middle section punch** (chungdan bahndae ahp joomok chirugi).

19: Maintain stance. Execute a right **middle section front punch** (chungdan ahp joomok chirugi).

20: Step right foot back toward **A** into a **left foot forward back stance** (wen bal dwi sogi) executing a left **lower section double knifehand block** (hadan dool sohn-kal makgi).

20, Continued

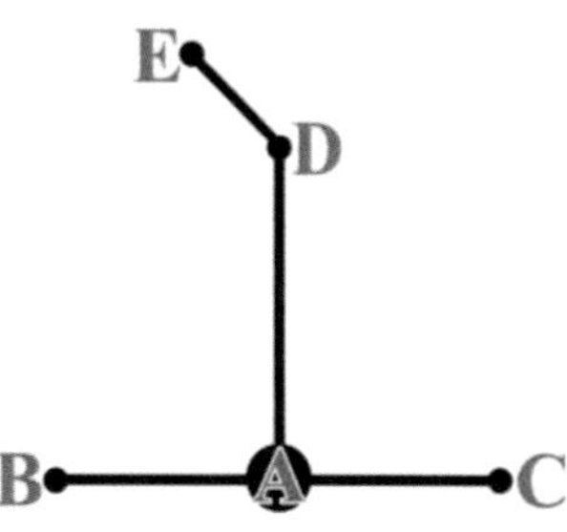

21: Shift out with the left foot into a **left foot forward front stance** (wen bal ahp sogi) and execute a right **reverse middle section punch** (chungdan bahndae ahp joomok chirugi).

22: Maintain stance. Execute a left **middle section front punch** (chungdan ahp joomok chirugi).

23: Step left foot back toward **A** forming a **right foot forward back stance** (orun bal dwi sogi). Execute a right **lower section forearm block** (hadan palmok makgi).

23, Continued

24: Step backward toward **A** forming a **left foot forward back stance** (wen bal dwi sogi). Execute a left **lower section forearm block** (hadan palmok makgi).

24, Continued

25: Step toward **B** with left foot forming a **horse stance** (Kima sogi) and guarding to the left with a **guarding block** (daebi makgi).

25, Continued

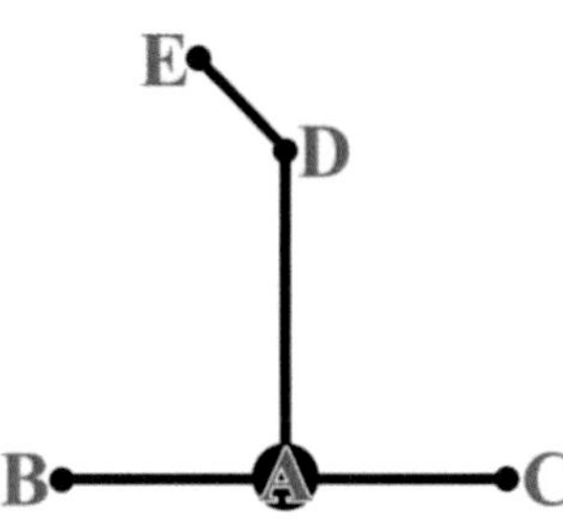

26: Move toward **B** with a left **step behind side thrust kick** (bal-diro omgyo yup chagi). Land in a **horse stance** (kima sogi) and immediately execute number 27.

26, Continued

26, Continued

27: Maintain stance. Execute a **high section outward knifehand strike** (sahngdan bakuro sohn-kal darigi) with the left hand.

27, Continued

28: Look over your right shoulder toward **C**. Bring left foot to right in a transitional **closed stance** (moa sogi). Step out toward **C** with right foot into a **horse stance** (kima sogi) while executing a **guarding block** (daebi makgi) toward **C**.

28, Continued

28, Continued

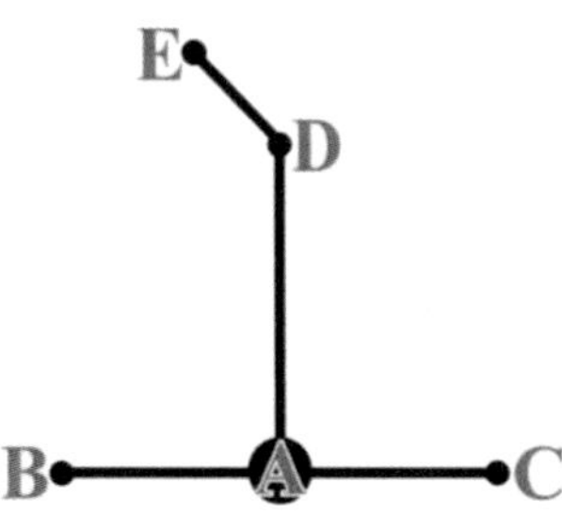

29: Move toward **C** with a right **step behind side thrust kick** (bal-diro omgyo yup chagi). Land in a **horse stance** (kima sogi) and immediately execute number 30.

29, Continued

29, Continued

30: Maintain stance. Execute a **high section outward knifehand strike** (sahngdan bakuro sohn-kal darigi) with the right hand. **Kihap.**

30, Continued

***Paro:*** Return Right Foot to Closed Stance, AKF Hand Position.

<u>Students testing for green stripe must know form Kyuki Il Chang.</u>

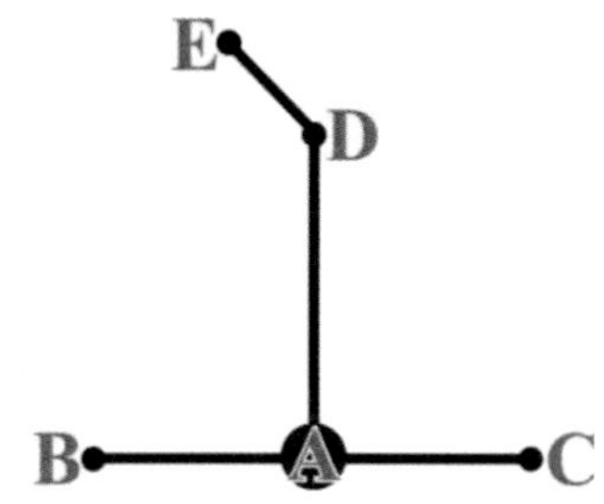


**Kyuki Il Chang:** **Spark Spirit.** Kyuki-Do's ability to awaken the spiritual potential within each of us.

**Ready Position:** Closed stance AKF hand position at A facing D.

**Movements:**

1: Begin by stepping toward **B**, forming a **left foot forward back stance** (wen bal dwi sogi) while executing a left **middle section double knifehand block** (chungdan dool sohn-kal makgi). **Kihap**.

2: Shift left foot toward **B**, forming **left foot forward front stance** (wen bal ahp sogi) while executing a right **reverse middle section knifehand block** (chungdan bahndae sohn-kal makgi).

3: Hook right hand and step with left foot onto line **AB** into a **horse stance** (kima sogi). Execute a left **outside forearm strike** (pakat palmok darigi) to the elbow.

4: Shift left foot to right into a transitional **closed stance** (moa sogi). Step out with right foot into a **right foot forward back stance** (orun bal dwi sogi) while executing a right **middle section double knifehand block** (chungdan dool sohn-kal makgi).

5: Shift right foot toward **C**, forming **right foot forward front stance** (orun bal ahp sogi) while executing a left **reverse middle section knifehand block** (chungdan bahndae sohn-kal makgi).

6: Hook left hand and step with right foot onto line **AC** into a **horse stance** (kima sogi). Execute a right **outside forearm strike** (pakat palmok darigi) to the elbow.

7: Shift right foot to left foot into a transitional **closed stance** (moa sogi). Step out with left foot toward **D**, forming a **left foot forward back stance** (wen bal dwi sogi) while executing a left **middle section double knifehand block** (chungdan dool sohn-kal makgi).

8: Shift left foot toward **D**, forming a **left foot forward front stance** (wen bal ahp sogi). Reach out with left hand and grab opponent's head. Execute a right **reverse high section front elbow strike** (sahngdan bahndae ahp palkumchi darigi) with your right elbow coming to meet your left hand.

9: Step forward with your right foot into a **right foot forward back stance** (orun bal dwi sogi) while executing a right **middle section double knifehand block** (chungdan dool sohn-kal makgi).

10: Shift right foot toward **D**, forming a **right foot forward front stance** (orun bal ahp sogi). Reach out with right hand and grab opponent's head. Execute a left **reverse high section front elbow strike** (sahngdan bahndae ahp palkumchi darigi) with your left elbow coming to meet your right hand.

11: Step forward toward **D**, forming a **left foot forward front stance** (wen bal ahp sogi). Execute a left **middle section front punch** (chungdan ahp joomok chirugi).

12: Maintain stance. Execute a right **reverse middle section front punch** (chungdan bahndae ahp joomok chirugi). **Kihap.**

13: Look to your left at a 45-degree angle toward **E**, and bring your hands up to a **guarding position** (daebi makgi). Execute a **roundhouse kick** (tollyo chagi) with your right leg. Land in a **right foot forward front stance** (orun bal ahp sogi) facing **E**. Immediately execute number 14.

14: Maintain stance and execute a right **middle section knifehand block** (chungdan sohn-kal makgi).

15: Maintain stance and execute a left **reverse high section palm heel strike** (sahngdan bahndae sohn-bahdahk chirugi).

16: Maintain stance and execute a right **high section palm heel strike** (sahngdan sohn-bahdahk chirugi). **Kihap.**

17: Stepping backwards toward **A,** bring right foot to left foot forming a transitional **closed stance** (moa sogi). Step back with left foot into a **right foot forward back stance** (orun bal dwi sogi) executing a right **lower section double knifehand block** (hadan dool sohn-kal makgi).

18: Shift out with the right foot into a **right foot forward front stance** (orun bal ahp sogi) and execute a left **reverse middle section punch** (chungdan bahndae ahp joomok chirugi).

19: Maintain stance. Execute a right **middle section front punch** (chungdan ahp joomok chirugi).

20: Step right foot back toward **A** into a **left foot forward back stance** (wen bal dwi sogi) executing a left **lower section double knifehand block** (hadan dool sohn-kal makgi).

21: Shift out with the left foot into a **left foot forward front stance** (wen bal ahp sogi) and execute a right **reverse middle section punch** (chungdan bahndae ahp joomok chirugi).

22: Maintain stance. Execute a left **middle section front punch** (chungdan ahp joomok chirugi).

23: Step left foot back toward **A** forming a **right foot forward back stance** (orun bal dwi sogi). Execute a right **lower section forearm block** (hadan palmok makgi).

24: Step backward toward **A** forming a **left foot forward back stance** (wen bal dwi sogi). Execute a left **lower section forearm block** (hadan palmok makgi).

25: Step toward **B** with left foot forming a **horse stance** (Kima sogi) and guarding to the left with a **guarding block** (daebi makgi).

26: Move toward **B** with a left **step behind side thrust kick** (bal-diro omgyo yup chagi). Land in a **horse stance** (kima sogi) and immediately execute number 27.

27: Maintain stance. Execute a **high section outward knifehand strike** (sahngdan bakuro sohn-kal darigi) with the left hand.

28: Look over your right shoulder toward **C**. Bring left foot to right in a transitional **closed stance** (moa sogi). Step out toward **C** with right foot into a **horse stance** (kima sogi) while executing a **guarding block** (daebi makgi) toward **C**.

29: Move toward **C** with a right **step behind side thrust kick** (bal-diro omgyo yup chagi). Land in a **horse stance** (kima sogi) and immediately execute number 30.

30: Maintain stance. Execute a **high section outward knifehand strike** (sahngdan bakuro sohn-kal darigi) with the right hand. **Kihap.**

***Paro:*** Return Right Leg to Ready Position.

# 격기이장

# Kyuki Yee Chang

(31 Movements)
Presented by Head Master Tim Mullis

**Kyuki Yee Chang:** **Spark Mental.** Kyuki-Do's ability to awaken the mental potential within each of us.

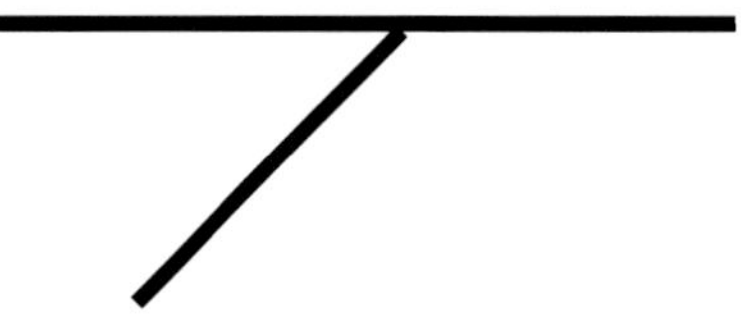

**Ready Position:** Closed Stance AKF Hand Position.

1: Step left foot back toward **B** to form a **right foot forward back stance** (orun bal dwi sogi). Execute a right **middle section inside forearm block** (chungdan ahn palmok makgi). **Kihap.**

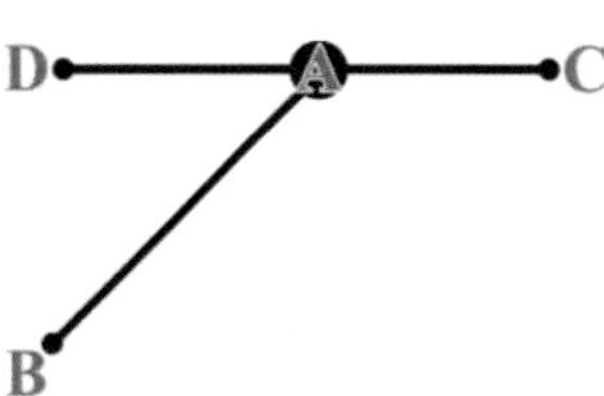

2: Maintain stance and execute a right hand **low section palm heel block** (hadan sohn-bahdahk makgi).

3: Maintain stance and execute a left **reverse middle section turning punch** (chungdan bahndae tollyo ahp joomok chirugi).

4: Step right leg back toward **B** to form a **left foot forward back stance** (wen bal dwi sogi). Execute a left **middle section inside forearm block** (chungdan ahn palmok makgi).

5: Maintain stance and execute a left hand **low section palm heel block** (hadan sohn-bahdahk makgi).

6: Maintain stance and execute a right **reverse middle section turning punch** (chungdan bahndae tollyo ahp joomok chirugi).

7: Step counterclockwise 180-degrees with the left foot, forming a **horse stance** (kima sogi) along line **AB**. Execute a **middle section twin inside forearm block** (chungdan sahng ahn palmok makgi).

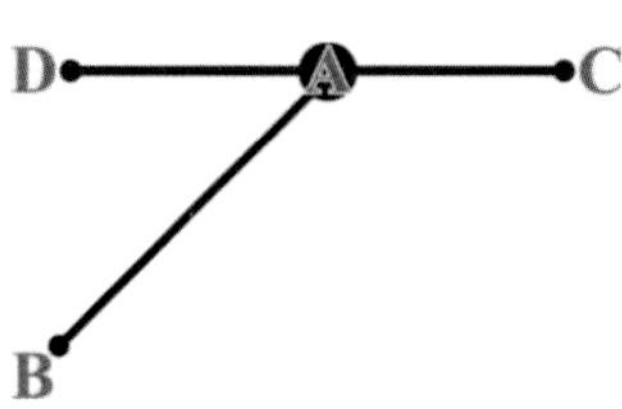


8: Step counterclockwise with the left foot 180-degrees toward **A**, forming a **horse stance** (Kima sogi) along line **AB**. Execute a right **high section backfist strike** (sahngdan deung joomok chirugi) while simultaneously executing a left **low section forearm block** (hadan palmok makgi).

8, Continued

9: Move right leg counterclockwise 180-degrees toward **A**, forming a **right foot forward fixed stance** (orun bal kojung sogi). Execute a right **middle section side punch** (chungdan yup joomok chirugi). **Kihap.**

9, Continued

10: Step counterclockwise with left foot toward **C**, landing in a **left foot forward back stance** (wen bal dwi sogi) facing **C**. Execute a left **middle section inside forearm block** (chungdan ahn palmok makgi).

11: Maintain stance and execute a left hand **low section palm heel block** (hadan sohn-bahdahk makgi).

12: Maintain stance and execute a right **reverse middle section turning punch** (chungdan bahndae tollyo ahp joomok chirugi).

13: Step right leg forward toward **C** to form a **right foot forward back stance** (orun bal dwi sogi). Execute a right **middle section inside forearm block** (chungdan ahn palmok makgi).

14: Maintain stance and execute a right hand **low section palm heel block** (hadan sohn-bahdahk makgi).

15: Maintain stance and execute a left **reverse middle section turning punch** (chungdan bahndae tollyo ahp joomok chirugi).

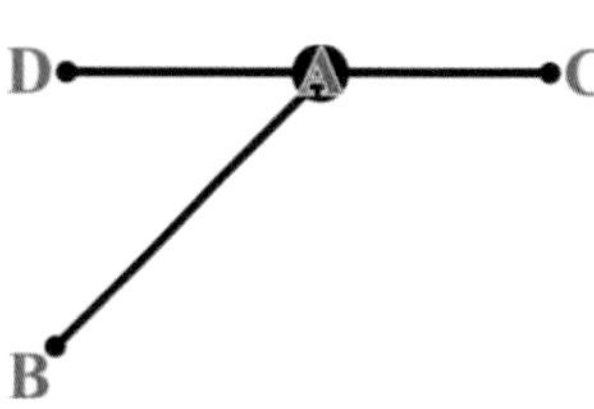

16: Step clockwise 180-degrees with the left foot, forming a **horse stance** (kima sogi) along line **AC**. Execute a **middle section twin inside forearm block** (chungdan sahng ahn palmok makgi).

17: Step clockwise with the left foot 180-degrees toward **A**, forming a **horse stance** (kima sogi) along line **AC**. Execute a right **high section backfist strike** (sahngdan deung joomok chirugi) while simultaneously executing a left **low section forearm block** (hadan palmok makgi).

17, Continued

18: Step right foot forward toward **A** to form a **right foot forward back stance** (orun bal dwi sogi). Stack and execute a **twin forearm box block** (sahng sohn palmok makgi). See #20 for proper stack position.

18, Continued

19: Maintain stance and execute a left **reverse middle section uppercut strike** (chungdan bahndae twijibo chirugi), bringing your right fist to your left shoulder.

19, Continued

20: Step left foot forward toward **D** to form a **left foot forward back stance** (wen bal dwi sogi). Stack and execute a **twin forearm box block** (sahng sohn palmok makgi). Note: palms together during stack.

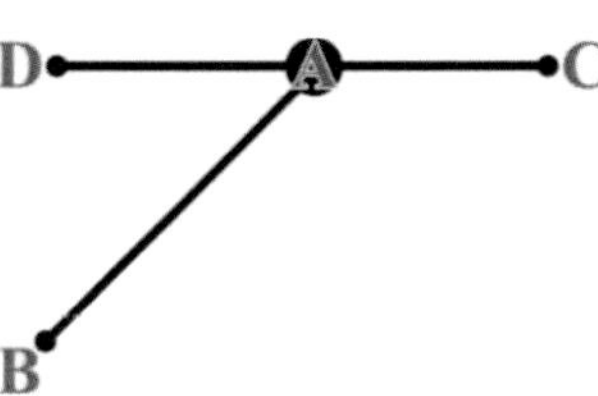

20, Continued

21: Maintain stance and execute a right **reverse middle section uppercut strike** (chungdan bahndae twijibo chirugi), bringing your left fist to your right shoulder.

21, Continued

22: Step forward into a **right foot forward front stance** (orun bal ahp sogi) executing an **augmented block** (kodoro makgi) to the right. (See #25 for proper stack position)

22, Continued

23: Maintain stance. Execute a left **reverse lower section forearm block** (bahndae hadan palmok makgi).

24: Retract right arm, raise right foot slightly, land in same stance and execute a **right high section front punch** (sahngdan ahp joomok chirugi).

24, Continued

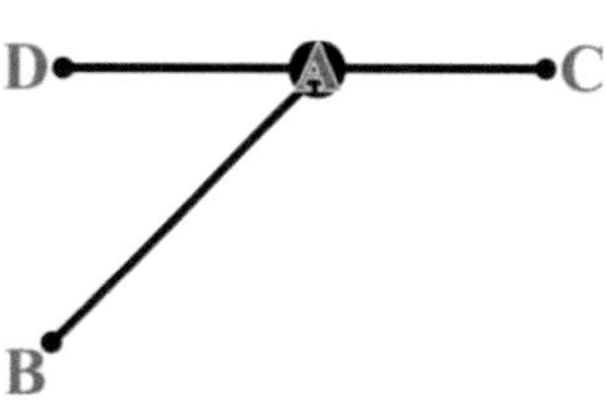

25: Step forward into a **left foot forward front stance** (wen bal ahp sogi) executing an **augmented block** (kodoro makgi) to the left. Note: palms both down during stack.

25, Continued

26: Maintain stance. Execute a right **reverse lower section forearm block** (bahndae hadan palmok makgi).

27: Retract left arm, raise left foot slightly, land in same stance and execute a left **high section front punch** (sahngdan ahp joomok chirugi).

27, Continued

28: Step left foot over to the right and pivot on the balls of your feet 180-degrees toward **A**, forming a **right foot forward front stance** (orun bal ahp sogi) facing **A**. Execute a **wedging knifehand block** (hecho sohn-kal makgi).

28, Continued

28, Continued

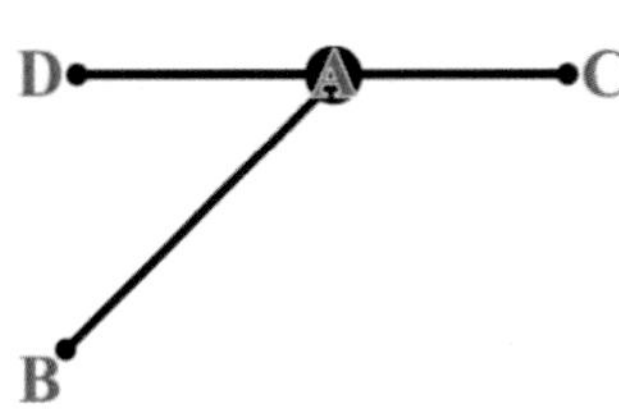

29: Step forward with left foot into a **left foot forward front stance** (wen bal ahp sogi), executing a right **reverse high section upward elbow strike** (sahngdan bahndae wi palkumchi darigi) with the right elbow.

30: Step onto line **DC** with right foot forming a **horse stance** (kima sogi) facing front. Execute a **middle section twin rear elbow strike** (chungdan sahng dwi palkumchi darigi).

30, Continued

31: Maintain stance and execute a **high section twin punch** (sahngdan sahng ahp joomok chirugi) with the fists at a 45-degree angle. **Kihap.**

***Paro:*** Return Right Leg to Ready Position.

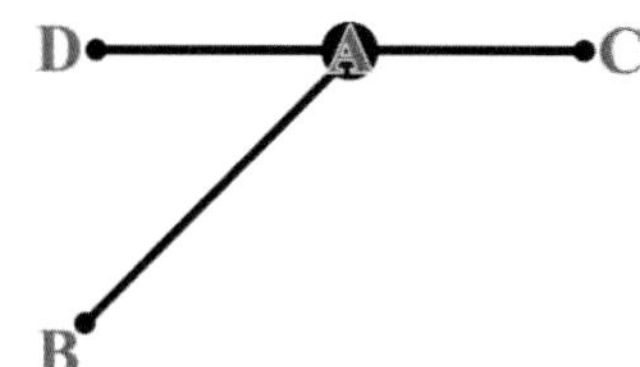


<u>Students testing for green belt must know form Kyuki Yee Chang.</u>

**Kyuki Yee Chang: Spark Mental.** Kyuki-Do's ability to awaken the mental potential within each of us.

**Ready Position:** Closed stance AKF hand position at A facing forward.

**Movements:**

1: Step left foot back toward **B** to form a **right foot forward back stance** (orun bal dwi sogi). Execute a right **middle section inside forearm block** (chungdan ahn palmok makgi). **Kihap.**

2: Maintain stance and execute a right hand **low section palm heel block** (hadan sohn-bahdahk makgi).

3: Maintain stance and execute a left **reverse middle section turning punch** (chungdan bahndae tollyo ahp joomok chirugi).

4: Step right leg back toward **B** to form a **left foot forward back stance** (wen bal dwi sogi). Execute a left **middle section inside forearm block** (chungdan ahn palmok makgi).

5: Maintain stance and execute a left hand **low section palm heel block** (hadan sohn-bahdahk makgi).

6: Maintain stance and execute a right **reverse middle section turning punch** (chungdan bahndae tollyo ahp joomok chirugi).

7: Step counterclockwise 180-degrees with the left foot, forming a **horse stance** (kima sogi) along line **AB**. Execute a **middle section twin inside forearm block** (chungdan sahng ahn palmok makgi).

8: Step counterclockwise with the left foot 180-degrees toward **A**, forming a **horse stance** (Kima sogi) along line **AB**. Execute a right **high section backfist strike** (sahngdan deung joomok chirugi) while simultaneously executing a left **low section forearm block** (hadan palmok makgi).

9: Move right leg counterclockwise 180-degrees toward **A**, forming a **right foot forward fixed stance** (orun bal kojung sogi). Execute a right **middle section side punch** (chungdan yup joomok chirugi). **Kihap.**

10: Step counterclockwise with left foot toward **C**, landing in a **left foot forward back stance** (wen bal dwi sogi) facing **C**. Execute a left **middle section inside forearm block** (chungdan ahn palmok makgi).

11: Maintain stance and execute a left hand **low section palm heel block** (hadan sohn-bahdahk makgi).

12: Maintain stance and execute a right **reverse middle section turning punch** (chungdan bahndae tollyo ahp joomok chirugi).

13: Step right leg forward toward **C** to form a **right foot forward back stance** (orun bal dwi sogi). Execute a right **middle section inside forearm block** (chungdan ahn palmok makgi).

14: Maintain stance and execute a right hand **low section palm heel block** (hadan sohn-bahdahk makgi).

15: Maintain stance and execute a left **reverse middle section turning punch** (chungdan bahndae tollyo ahp joomok chirugi).

16: Step clockwise 180-degrees with the left foot, forming a **horse stance** (kima sogi) along line **AC**. Execute a **middle section twin inside forearm block** (chungdan sahng ahn palmok makgi).

17: Step clockwise with the left foot 180-degrees toward **A**, forming a **horse stance** (kima sogi) along line **AC**. Execute a right **high section backfist strike** (sahngdan deung joomok chirugi) while simultaneously executing a left **low section forearm block** (hadan palmok makgi).

18: Step right foot forward toward **A** to form a **right foot forward back stance** (orun bal dwi sogi). Stack and execute a **twin forearm box block** (sahng sohn palmok makgi).

19: Maintain stance and execute a left **reverse middle section uppercut strike** (chungdan bahndae twijibo chirugi), bringing your right fist to your left shoulder.

20: Step left foot forward toward **D** to form a **left foot forward back stance** (wen bal dwi sogi). Stack and execute a **twin forearm box block** (sahng sohn palmok makgi).

21: Maintain stance and execute a right **reverse middle section uppercut strike** (chungdan bahndae twijibo chirugi), bringing your left fist to your right shoulder.

22: Step forward into a **right foot forward front stance** (orun bal ahp sogi) executing an **augmented block** (kodoro makgi) to the right.

23: Maintain stance. Execute a left **reverse lower section forearm block** (bahndae hadan palmok makgi).

24: Retract right arm, raise right foot slightly, land in same stance and execute a right **high section front punch** (sahngdan ahp joomok chirugi).

25: Step forward into a **left foot forward front stance** (wen bal ahp sogi) executing an **augmented block** (kodoro makgi) to the left.

26: Maintain stance. Execute a right **reverse lower section forearm block** (bahndae hadan palmok makgi).

27: Retract left arm, raise left foot slightly, land in same stance and execute a left **high section front punch** (sahngdan ahp joomok chirugi).

28: Step left foot over to the right and pivot on the balls of your feet foot 180-degrees toward **A**, forming a **right foot forward front stance** (orun bal ahp sogi) facing **A**. Execute a **wedging knifehand block** (hecho sohn-kal makgi).

29: Step forward with left foot into a **left foot forward front stance** (wen bal ahp sogi), executing a right **reverse high section upward elbow strike** (sahngdan bahndae wi palkumchi darigi) with the right elbow.

30: Step onto line **DC** with right foot forming a **horse stance** (kima sogi) facing front. Execute a **middle section twin rear elbow strike** (chungdan sahng dwi palkumchi darigi).

31: Maintain stance and execute a **high section twin punch** (sahngdan sahng ahp joomok chirugi) with the fists at a 45-degree angle. **Kihap.**

***Paro:*** Return Right Leg to Ready Position.

# 격기삼장

# Kyuki Sam Chang

(29 Movements)
Presented by Master Merrill Sinclair

**Kyuki Sam Chang:** **Spark Physical.** Kyuki-Do's ability to awaken the physical potential within each of us.

**Ready Position:** Closed Stance AKF Hand Position.

1: Right foot steps back toward **C** forming a **left foot forward front stance** (wen bal ahp sogi). Execute a left **middle section forearm block** (chungdan palmok makgi). **Kihap.**

2: Step back with left foot forming a **right foot forward front stance** (orun bal ahp sogi). Execute a right **high section palm heel strike** (sahngdan sohn-bahdahk chirugi).

3: Move forward executing a left **inside to outside crescent kick** (ahp yuk tollyo chagi). Continue immediately to movement 4.

3, Continued

4: Execute a right leg **roundhouse kick** (tollyo chagi). Continue immediately to movement 5.

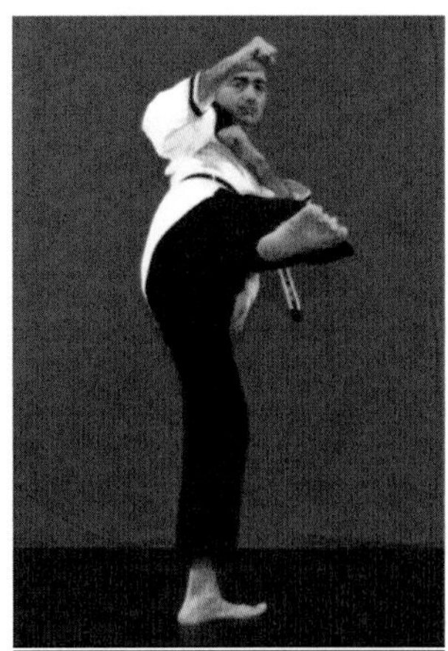

4, Continued

5: Turn 180 degrees counterclockwise toward **B**, executing a left leg **spinning side thrust kick** (dwi tollyo yup chagi). Land in a **left foot forward fixed stance** (wen bal kojung sogi) and immediately execute movement number 6.

5, Continued

6: Maintain stance and execute a left **high section outward knifehand strike** (sahngdan bakuro sohn-kal darigi).

6, Continued

7: Shift into a **left kneeling front stance** (wen bal murrup gurro sogi) facing **B** (right knee should be on the ground). Execute a combination left **high section knifehand block** (sahngdan sohn-kal makgi) and right **reverse uppercut strike** (bahndae twijibo chirugi). **Kihap.**

7, Continued

8: Move left hand around opponent's head and execute a right **reverse high section front elbow strike** to the head (sahngdan bahndae ahp palkumchi darigi). Bring the right elbow to the left hand; the right hand should end up over the left shoulder.

8, Continued

9: Reach up, grab opponent's head and pull downward, throwing opponent to the right at a 45-degree angle.

9, Continued

10: Turn 180-degrees to the right, shifting your weight from the right knee to the left knee. While still kneeling, execute a **low section kneeling spin side thrust kick** (hadan murrup gurro dwi tollyo yup chagi) with the right leg. You should be kneeling facing **C** while performing this kick.

B

A

C

10, Continued

10, Continued

11: Push yourself up backwards, forming a **left foot forward back stance** (wen bal dwi sogi), executing a **middle section twin palm heel pushing block** (chungdan sahng sohn-bahdahk miro makgi).

11, Alternate View

12: Step forward toward **A** into a **right foot forward front stance** (orun bal ahp sogi) and execute a **low section X-forearm block** (hadan kyocha palmok makgi).

12, Alternate View

13: Step forward toward **A** into a **left foot forward front stance** (wen bal ahp sogi) and execute a **high section X-forearm block** (sahngdan kyocha palmok makgi).

13, Alternate View

14: Step back with left foot into a **right foot forward front stance** (orun bal ahp sogi) and execute a right **middle section forearm block** (chungdan palmok makgi).

15: Step back with right foot into a **left foot forward front stance** (wen bal ahp sogi) and execute a left **high section palm heel strike** (sahngdan sohn-bahdahk chirugi).

16: Move forward executing a right **inside to outside crescent kick** (ahp yuk tollyo chagi). Continue immediately to movement 17.

16, Continued

17: Execute a left leg **roundhouse kick** (tollyo chagi). Continue immediately to movement 18.

17, Continued

18: Turn 180 degrees clockwise toward **C**, executing a right leg **spinning side thrust kick** (dwi tollyo yup chagi). Land in a **right foot forward fixed stance** (orun bal kojung sogi) and immediately execute movement number 19.

18, Continued

19: Maintain stance and execute a right **high section outward knifehand strike** (sahngdan bakuro sohn-kal darigi).

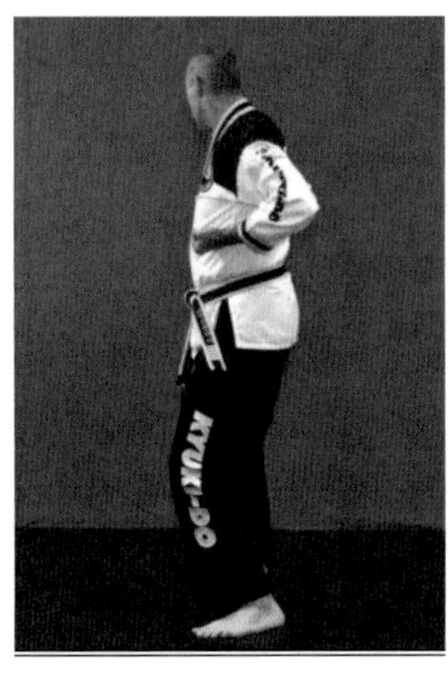

19, Continued

20: Shift into a **right kneeling front stance** (orun bal murrup gurro sogi) facing **B** (left knee should be on the ground). Execute a combination right **high section knifehand block** (sahngdan sohn-kal makgi) and left **reverse uppercut strike** (bahndae twijibo chirugi). **Kihap.**

20, Continued

21: Move right hand around opponent's head and execute a left **reverse high section front elbow strike** to the head (sahngdan bahndae ahp palkumchi darigi). Bring the left elbow to the right hand; the left hand should end up over the right shoulder.

21, Continued

22: Reach up, grab opponent's head and pull downward, throwing opponent to the left at a 45-degree angle.

22, Continued

23: Turn 180 degrees to the left, shifting your weight from the left knee to the right knee. While still kneeling, execute a **low section kneeling spin side thrust kick** (hadan murrup gurro dwi tollyo yup chagi) with the left leg. You should be kneeling facing **B** while performing this kick.

23, Continued

24: Push yourself up backwards, forming a **right foot forward back stance** (orun bal dwi sogi), executing a **middle section twin palm heel pushing block** (chungdan sahng sohn-bahdahk miro makgi).

25: Step forward toward **A** into a **left foot forward front stance** (wen bal ahp sogi) and execute a **low section X-forearm block** (hadan kyocha palmok makgi).

26: Step forward toward **A** into a **right foot forward front stance** (orun bal ahp sogi) and execute a **high section X-forearm block** (sahngdan kyocha palmok makgi).

27: Execute a low section left leg **twisting kick** (hadan bpi-turyo chagi).

27, Continued (Note that the kick targets the hip or lower)

27, Continued

28: Set the kicking leg down into a **left foot forward front stance** (wen bal ahp sogi) and execute a left **high section front punch** (sahngdan ahp joomok chirugi).

29: Maintain stance and execute a **reverse middle section punch** (chungdan bahndae ahp joomok chirugi). **Kihap.**

***Paro:*** Left Foot Steps Back to Ready Position.

Students testing for blue stripe must know form Kyuki Sam Chang.

B
A
C

**Kyuki Sam Chang:** **Spark Physical.** Kyuki-Do's ability to awaken the physical potential within each of us.

**Ready Position:** Closed stance AKF hand position at A facing B.

**Movements:**

1: Right foot steps back toward **C** forming a **left foot forward front stance** (wen bal ahp sogi). Execute a left **middle section forearm block** (chungdan palmok makgi). **Kihap.**

2: Step back with left foot forming a **right foot forward front stance** (orun bal ahp sogi). Execute a right **high section palm heel strike** (sahngdan sohn-bahdahk chirugi).

3: Move forward executing a left **inside to outside crescent kick** (ahp yuk tollyo chagi). Continue immediately to movement 4.

4: Execute a right leg **roundhouse kick** (tollyo chagi). Continue immediately to movement 5.

5: Turn 180 degrees counterclockwise toward **B**, executing a left leg **spinning side thrust kick** (dwi tollyo yup chagi). Land in a **left foot forward fixed stance** (wen bal kojung sogi) and immediately execute movement number 6.

6: Maintain stance and execute a left **high section outward knifehand strike** (sahngdan bakuro sohn-kal darigi).

7: Shift into a **left kneeling front stance** (wen bal murrup gurro sogi) facing **B** (right knee should be on the ground). Execute a combination left **high section knifehand block** (sahngdan sohn-kal makgi) and right **reverse uppercut strike** (bahndae twijibo chirugi). **Kihap.**

8: Move left hand around opponent's head and execute a right **reverse high section front elbow strike** to the head (sahngdan bahndae ahp palkumchi darigi). Bring the right elbow to the left hand; the right hand should end up over the left shoulder.

9: Reach up, grab opponent's head and pull downward, throwing opponent to the right at a 45-degree angle.

10: Turn 180-degrees to the right, shifting your weight from the right knee to the left knee. While still kneeling, execute a **low section kneeling spin side thrust kick** (hadan murrup gurro dwi tollyo yup chagi) with the right leg. You should be kneeling facing **C** while performing this kick.

11: Push yourself up backwards, forming a **left foot forward back stance** (wen bal dwi sogi), executing a **middle section twin palm heel pushing block** (chungdan sahng sohn-bahdahk miro makgi).

12: Step forward toward **A** into a **right foot forward front stance** (orun bal ahp sogi) and execute a **low section X-forearm block** (hadan kyocha palmok makgi).

13: Step forward toward **A** into a **left foot forward front stance** (wen bal ahp sogi) and execute a **high section X-forearm block** (sahngdan kyocha palmok makgi).

14: Step back with left foot into a **right foot forward front stance** (orun bal ahp sogi) and execute a right **middle section forearm block** (chungdan palmok makgi).

15: Step back with right foot into a **left foot forward front stance** (wen bal ahp sogi) and execute a left **high section palm heel strike** (sahngdan sohn-bahdahk chirugi).

16: Move forward executing a right **inside to outside crescent kick** (ahp yuk tollyo chagi). Continue immediately to movement 17.

17: Execute a left leg **roundhouse kick** (tollyo chagi). Continue immediately to movement 18.

18: Turn 180 degrees clockwise toward **C**, executing a right leg **spinning side thrust kick** (dwi tollyo yup chagi). Land in a **right foot forward fixed stance** (orun bal kojung sogi) and immediately execute movement number 19.

19: Maintain stance and execute a right **high section outward knifehand strike** (sahngdan bakuro sohn-kal darigi).

20: Shift into a **right kneeling front stance** (orun bal murrup gurro sogi) facing **B** (left knee should be on the ground). Execute a combination right **high section knifehand block** (sahngdan sohn-kal makgi) and left **reverse uppercut strike** (bahndae twijibo chirugi). **Kihap.**

21: Move right hand around opponent's head and execute a left **reverse high section front elbow strike** to the head (sahngdan bahndae ahp palkumchi darigi). Bring the left elbow to the right hand; the left hand should end up over the right shoulder.

22: Reach up, grab opponent's head and pull downward, throwing opponent to the left at a 45-degree angle.

23: Turn 180 degrees to the left, shifting your weight from the left knee to the right knee. While still kneeling, execute a **low section kneeling spin side thrust kick** (hadan murrup gurro dwi tollyo yup chagi) with the left leg. You should be kneeling facing **B** while performing this kick.

24: Push yourself up backwards, forming a **right foot forward back stance** (orun bal dwi sogi), executing a **middle section twin palm heel pushing block** (chungdan sahng sohn-bahdahk miro makgi).

25: Step forward toward **A** into a **left foot forward front stance** (wen bal ahp sogi) and execute a **low section X-forearm block** (hadan kyocha palmok makgi).

26: Step forward toward **A** into a **right foot forward front stance** (orun bal ahp sogi) and execute a **high section X-forearm block** (sahngdan kyocha palmok makgi).

27: Execute a low section left leg **twisting kick** (hadan bpi-turyo chagi).

28: Set the kicking leg down into a **left foot forward front stance** (wen bal ahp sogi) and execute a left **high section front punch** (sahngdan ahp joomok chirugi).

29: Maintain stance and execute a **reverse middle section punch** (chungdan bahndae ahp joomok chirugi). **Kihap.**

***Paro:*** Return Left Leg to Ready Position.

# 근본

# Guen Bon

(28 Movements)
Presented by Master Nicole Holden Arendt

**Guen Bon:** **Roots.** Representing the past experiences of those who have gone before us and given of themselves for our benefit.

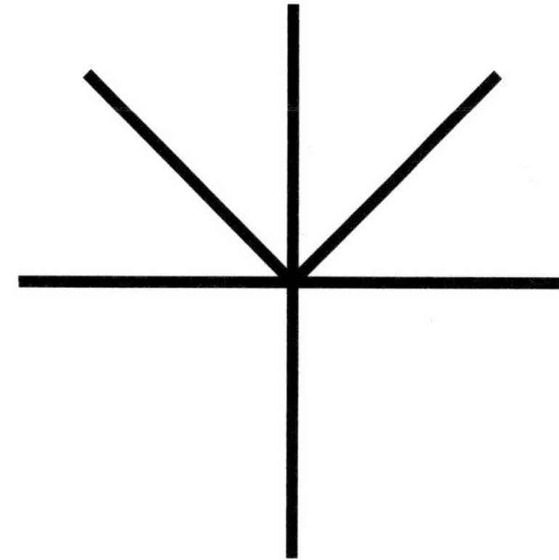

**Ready Position:** Parallel Stance Double Arc Hand Pressing Earth

1: Step back with right leg toward **B** forming a **left foot forward front stance** (wen bal ahp sogi). Execute a **left low section forearm block/right reverse middle section inside forearm block** (hadan palmok makgi/chungdan bahndae ahn palmok makgi). **Kihap.**

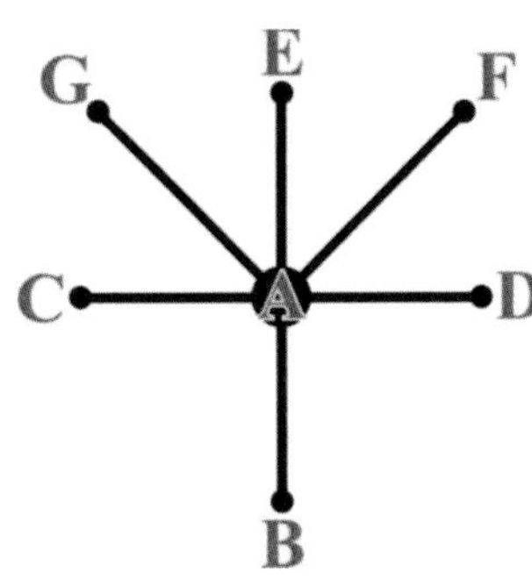


2: Step back with left leg into a **right foot forward front stance** (orun bal ahp sogi). Execute a **right low section forearm block/left reverse middle section inside forearm block** (hadan palmok makgi/chungdan bahndae ahn palmok makgi).

3: Step forward with left leg into a **left foot forward back stance** (wen bal dwi sogi) and execute a left **low section Kyuki-Do block** (hadan Kyuki-Do makgi).

3, Continued

3, Alternate View (note position and orientation of back hand.)

4: Shift right foot to left foot into a transitional **closed stance** (moa sogi). Step out with left foot toward **C** forming a **left foot forward back stance** (wen bal dwi sogi). Stack and execute a **modified box block** (byun gyun sahng sohn palmok makgi).

4, Continued

5: Maintain stance and execute a right **reverse high section inward knifehand strike** (sahngdan bahndae anuro sohn-kal darigi) to the neck. Bring your left fist to your right shoulder.

5, Continued

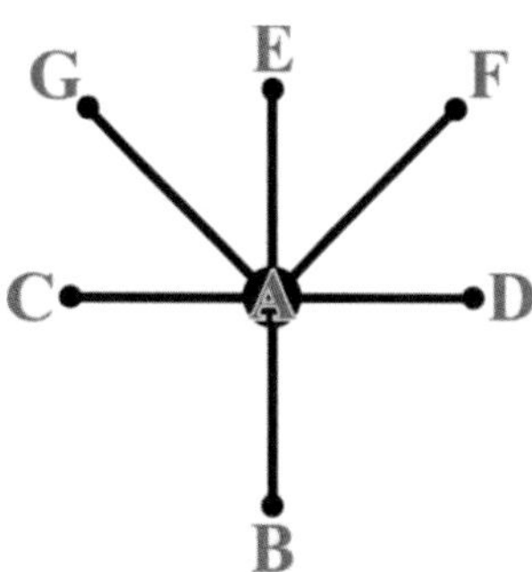

6: Maintain stance and execute a left **middle section side punch** (chungdan yup joomok chirugi). Initiate this punch by reaching forward with your right hand.

6, Continued

7: Step forward with right foot toward **C** to form a **right foot forward front stance** (orun bal ahp sogi) and execute a right **middle section front punch** (chungdan ahp joomok chirugi).

8: Turn clockwise 180-degrees toward **D** and form a **right foot forward back stance** (orun bal dwi sogi). Stack and execute a **modified box block** (byun gyun sahng sohn palmok makgi).

8, Continued

9: Maintain stance and execute a left **reverse high section inward knifehand strike** (sahngdan bahndae anuro sohn-kal darigi) to the neck. Bring your right fist to your left shoulder.

9, Continued

10: Maintain stance and execute a right **middle section side punch** (chungdan yup joomok chirugi). Initiate this punch by reaching forward with your left hand.

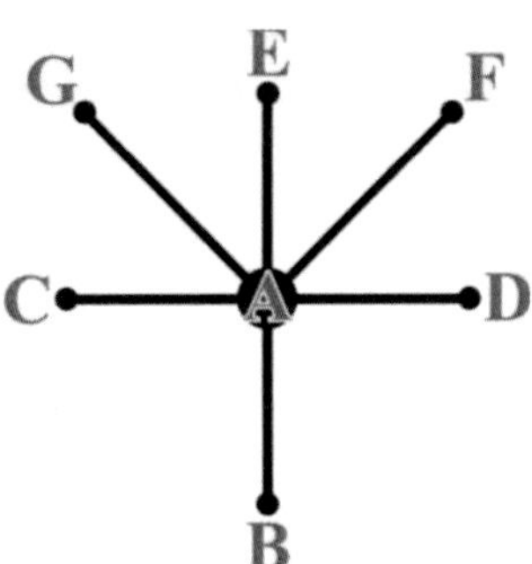

10, Continued

11: Step left foot forward toward **D** to form a **left foot forward front stance** (wen bal ahp sogi) and execute a left **middle section front punch** (chungdan ahp joomok chirugi).

12: Turn left 90-degrees toward **E** and form a **left foot forward back stance** (wen bal dwi sogi). Execute a **middle section double knifehand block** (chungdan dool sohn-kal makgi).

12, Continued

13: Step forward toward **E** with a right leg **front snap kick** (ahp chagi). Land in a transitional stance and immediately execute movement 14.

13, Continued

14: Move forward toward **E** with a left leg **roundhouse kick** (tollyo chagi). Land in a transitional stance and immediately execute movement 15.

14, Continued

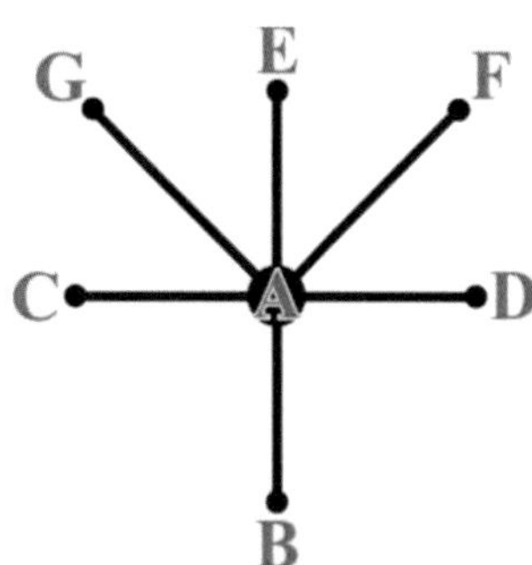

15: Moving forward toward **E** with a left leg **step behind side thrust kick** (bal-diro omgyo yup chagi) and land in a **left foot forward front stance** (wen bal ahp sogi). Immediately execute movement 16.

15, Continued

15, Continued

16: Maintain stance and execute a right **reverse high section downward hammerfist strike** (sahngdan bahndae naeryo meh joomok darigi). **Kihap.**

17: Step backward with left foot forming a **right foot forward front stance** (orun bal ahp sogi) and execute right **middle section knifehand block** (chungdan sohn-kal makgi).

18: Execute a right lead leg **front snap kick** (ahp chagi) and set the kicking leg down behind you forming a **left foot forward front stance** (wen bal ahp sogi).

18, Continued

19: Maintain stance and execute a left **middle section knifehand block** (chungdan sohn-kal makgi).

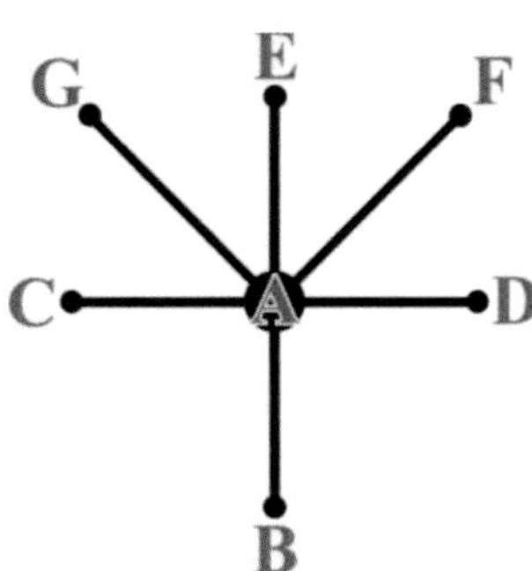

20: Execute a left lead leg **front snap kick** (ahp chagi), setting the kicking leg down behind you and pivoting on right foot counterclockwise onto line **AE**.

20, Continued

21: Land in a **horse stance** (kima sogi) and execute a **middle section double knifehand block** (chungdan dool sohn-kal makgi) toward **A.**

21, Continued

21, Alternate View

22: Execute a left **step behind side thrust kick** (bal-diro omgyo yup chagi) toward **A**. Land at **A** and bring left leg to right leg in a transitional **closed stance** (moa sogi). Note that your hands close to fists as you start.

22, Continued

22, Continued

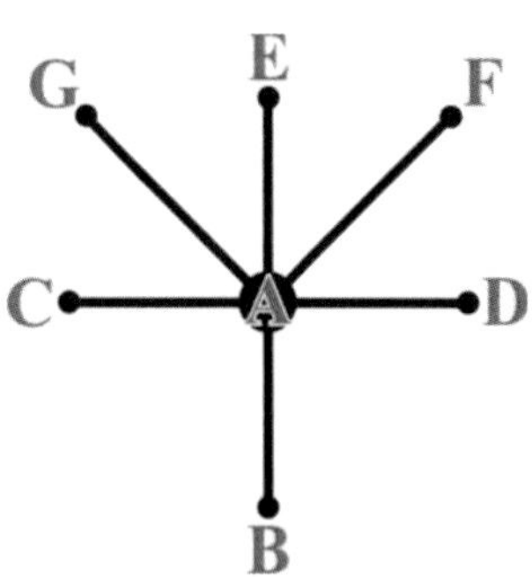

23: Step out with right foot 45-degrees toward **F**, forming a **right foot forward front stance** (orun bal ahp sogi). Execute a **wedging knifehand block** (hecho sohn-kal makgi).

23, Continued (note the chambering position of hands)

23, Continued

24: Grab right hand with left hand and execute a left **middle section knee strike** (chungdan murrup chirugi).

24, Continued (note that the hands do *not* contact the knee)

25: Step left foot back toward **A**, landing in a **horse stance** (kima sogi) along line **AF**. Execute a right **downward elbow strike** (naeryo palkumchi darigi) with your palm facing your body. **Kihap.**

26: Look 45-degrees toward **G**. Shift right foot to left foot forming a transitional **closed stance** (moa sogi). Step out with left foot 45-degrees toward **G**, forming a **left foot forward front stance** (wen bal ahp sogi). Execute a **wedging knifehand block** (hecho sohn-kal makgi).

26, Continued

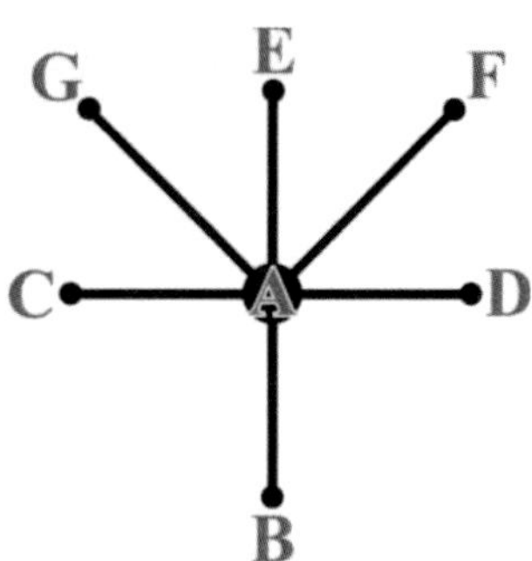


27: Grab left hand with right hand and execute a right **middle section knee strike** (chungdan murrup chirugi).

27, Continued (note that the hands do *not* contact the knee)

28: Step right foot back toward **A**, landing in a **horse stance** (kima sogi) along line **AG**. Execute a left **downward elbow strike** (naeryo palkumchi darigi) with your palm facing your body. **Kihap.**

***Paro:*** Return Left Leg to Ready Position.

Students testing for blue belt must know form Guen Bon.

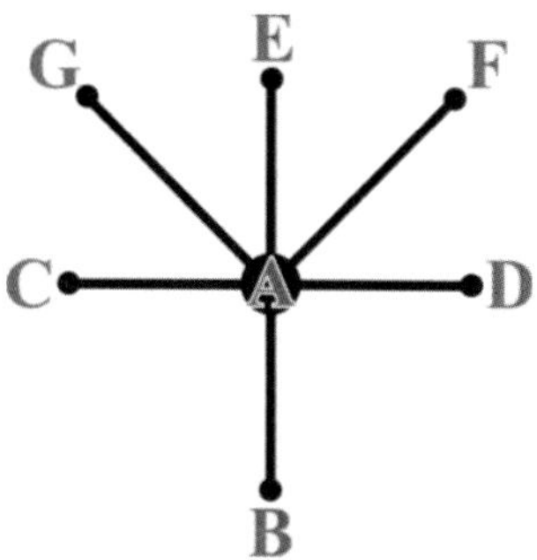


**Guen Bon: Roots.** Representing the past experiences of those who have gone before us and given of themselves for our benefit.
**Ready Position:** Parallel stance with double arc hand pressing earth at A facing E.
**Movements:**

1: Step back with right leg toward **B** forming a **left foot forward front stance** (wen bal ahp sogi). Execute a **left low section forearm block/right reverse middle section inside forearm block** (hadan palmok makgi/chungdan bahndae ahn palmok makgi). **Kihap.**

2: Step back with left leg into a **right foot forward front stance** (orun bal ahp sogi). Execute a **right low section forearm block/left reverse middle section inside forearm block** (hadan palmok makgi/chungdan bahndae ahn palmok makgi).

3: Step forward with left leg into a **left foot forward back stance** (wen bal dwi sogi) and execute a left **low section Kyuki-Do block** (hadan Kyuki-Do makgi).

4: Shift right foot to left foot into a transitional **closed stance** (moa sogi). Step out with left foot toward **C** forming a **left foot forward back stance** (wen bal dwi sogi). Stack and execute a **modified box block** (byun gyun sahng sohn palmok makgi).

5: Maintain stance and execute a right **reverse high section inward knifehand strike** (sahngdan bahndae anuro sohn-kal darigi) to the neck. Bring your left fist to your right shoulder.

6: Maintain stance and execute a left **middle section side punch** (chungdan yup joomok chirugi).

7: Step forward with right foot toward **C** to form a **right foot forward front stance** (orun bal ahp sogi) and execute a right **middle section front punch** (chungdan ahp joomok chirugi).

8: Turn clockwise 180-degrees toward **D** and form a **right foot forward back stance** (orun bal dwi sogi). Stack and execute a **modified box block** (byun gyun sahng sohn palmok makgi).

9: Maintain stance and execute a left **reverse high section inward knifehand strike** (sahngdan bahndae anuro sohn-kal darigi) to the neck. Bring your left fist to your right shoulder.

10: Maintain stance and execute a right **middle section side punch** (chungdan yup joomok chirugi).

11: Step left foot forward toward **D** to form a **left foot forward front stance** (wen bal ahp sogi) and execute a left **middle section front punch** (chungdan ahp joomok chirugi).

12: Turn left 90-degrees toward **E** and form a **left foot forward back stance** (wen bal dwi sogi). Execute a **middle section double knifehand block** (chungdan dool sohn-kal makgi).

13: Step forward toward **E** with a right leg **front snap kick** (ahp chagi). Land in a transitional stance and immediately execute movement 14.

14: Move forward toward **E** with a left leg **roundhouse kick** (tollyo chagi). Land in a transitional stance and immediately execute movement 15.

15: Moving forward toward **E** with a left leg **step behind side thrust kick** (bal-diro omgyo yup chagi) and land in a **left foot forward front stance** (wen bal ahp sogi). Immediately execute movement 16.

16: Maintain stance and execute a right **reverse high section downward hammerfist strike** (sahngdan bahndae naeryo meh joomok darigi). **Kihap.**

17: Step backward with left foot forming a **right foot forward front stance** (orun bal ahp sogi) and execute right **middle section knifehand block** (chungdan sohn-kal makgi).

18: Execute a right lead leg **front snap kick** (ahp chagi) and set the kicking leg down behind you, forming a **left foot forward front stance** (wen bal ahp sogi).

19: Maintain stance and execute a left **middle section knifehand block** (chungdan sohn-kal makgi).

20: Execute a left lead leg **front snap kick** (ahp chagi), setting the kicking leg down behind you and pivoting on right foot counterclockwise onto line **AE**.

21: Land in a **horse stance** (kima sogi) and execute a **middle section double knifehand block** (chungdan dool sohn-kal makgi) toward **A.**

22: Execute a left **step behind side thrust kick** (bal-diro omgyo yup chagi) toward **A**. Land at **A** and bring left leg to right leg in a transitional **closed stance** (moa sogi). Note that your hands close as you start.

23: Step out with right foot 45-degrees toward **F**, forming a **right foot forward front stance** (orun bal ahp sogi). Execute a **wedging knifehand block** (hecho sohn-kal makgi).

24: Grab right hand with left hand and execute a left **middle section knee strike** (chungdan murrup chirugi).

25: Step left foot back toward **A**, landing in a **horse stance** (kima sogi) along line **AF**. Execute a right **downward elbow strike** (naeryo palkumchi darigi) with your palm facing your body. **Kihap.**

26: Look 45-degrees toward **G**. Shift right foot to left foot forming a transitional **closed stance** (moa sogi). Step out with left foot 45-degrees toward **G**, forming a **left foot forward front stance** (wen bal ahp sogi). Execute a **wedging knifehand block** (hecho sohn-kal makgi).

27: Grab left hand with right hand and execute a right **middle section knee strike** (chungdan murrup chirugi).

28: Step right foot back toward **A**, landing in a **horse stance** (kima sogi) along line **AG**. Execute a left **downward elbow strike** (naeryo palkumchi darigi) with your palm facing your body. **Kihap.**

***Paro:*** Return Left Leg to Ready Position.

# 천지인일장

# Chonji In Il Chang

(33 Movements)
Presented by Master Christine Bjorkquist

**Chon Ji In Il Chang:** **Sky.** The limitless potential for the development and well-being of the individual.

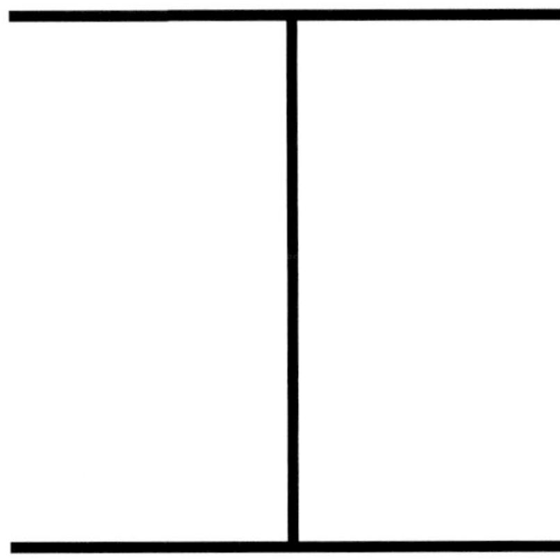

**Ready Position:** Parallel Stance Pushing High Section Double Arc Hand.

1: Step left foot 90-degrees toward **B** forming a **left foot forward back stance** (wen bal dwi sogi). Execute a left **middle section corkscrew trap, in to out** (kamuh toe olgami) taking care that the circle is large enough to trap an opponent's arm. **Kihap**.

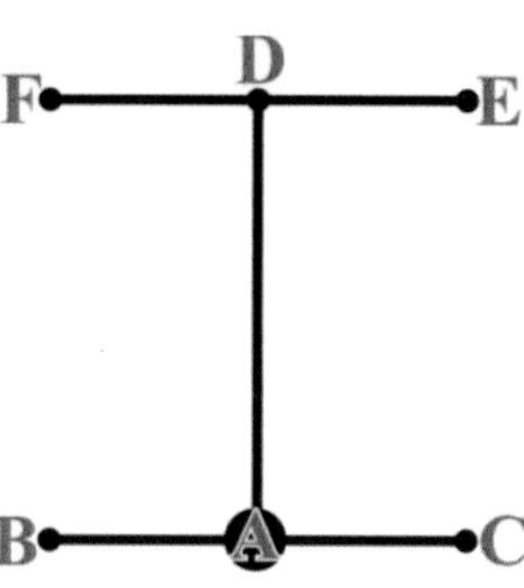

1, Continued

1, Continued

2: Maintain trap and shift left foot, forming a **left foot forward front stance** (wen bal ahp sogi) facing **B**. Execute a right **reverse high section palm heel strike** (sahngdan bahndae sohn-bahdahk chirugi).

3: Maintain stance and execute a right **reverse low section palm heel strike** (hadan bahndae sohn-bahdahk chirugi) to the groin.

4: Shift from a left foot forward front stance to a **left foot forward back stance** (wen bal dwi sogi). Simultaneously execute a left **middle section palm heel pushing block** (chungdan sohn-bahdahk miro makgi) while bringing right fist up to guard the side of your face (olgool makgi).

5: Step forward toward **B** forming a **right foot forward front stance** (orun bal ahp sogi) and execute a right **middle section front punch** (chungdan ahp joomok chirugi).

6: Turn clockwise 180-degrees toward **C** forming a **right foot forward back stance** (orun bal dwi sogi). Execute a right **middle section corkscrew trap, in to out** (kamuh toe olgami) taking care that the circle is large enough to trap an opponent's arm.

6, Continued

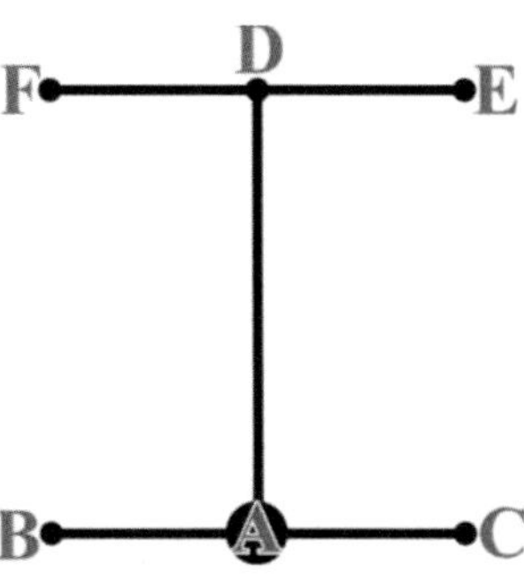


6, Continued

6, Continued

7: Maintain trap and shift right foot, forming a **right foot forward front stance** (orun bal ahp sogi) facing **C**. Execute a left **reverse high section palm heel strike** (sahngdan bahndae sohn-bahdahk chirugi).

8: Maintain stance and execute a left **reverse low section palm heel** (hadan bahndae sohn-bahdahk chirugi) to the groin.

9: Shift from a right foot forward front stance to a **right foot forward back stance** (orun bal dwi sogi). Simultaneously execute a right **middle section palm heel pushing block** (chungdan sohn-bahdahk miro makgi) while bringing left fist up to guard the side of your face (olgool makgi).

10: Step forward toward **C** forming a **left foot forward front stance** (wen bal ahp sogi) and execute a left **middle section front punch** (chungdan ahp joomok chirugi).

11: Step left foot 90-degrees toward **D** to form a **left foot forward front stance** (wen bal ahp sogi) and execute a **low section X-forearm block** (hadan kyocha palmok makgi).

12: Step forward with the right foot onto line **AD** and form a **horse stance** (kima sogi). Execute a right **outer forearm block** (pakat palmok makgi).

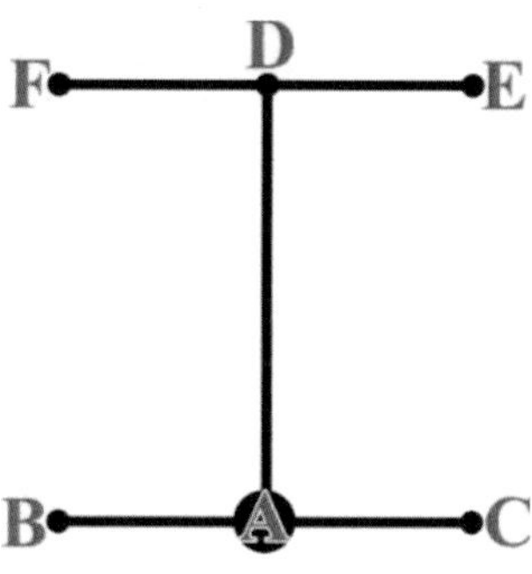

12, Alternate View

13: Execute a right leg **step behind side thrust kick** (bal-diro omgyo yup chagi) toward **D**.

13, Continued

13, Continued

14: Land in a **horse stance** (kima sogi) and execute a right **middle section augmented side elbow strike** (chungdan yup palkumchi churigi) toward **D**. **Kihap**.

14, Alternate View

15: Pivot counterclockwise with your left foot toward **E**, forming a **left foot forward front stance** (wen bal ahp sogi) and executing a left **middle section augmented forearm block** (chungdan kodoro makgi).

16: Maintain stance, execute a right **reverse high section spearhand strike** (sahngdan bahndae sohn-gut chirugi) with your palm downward.

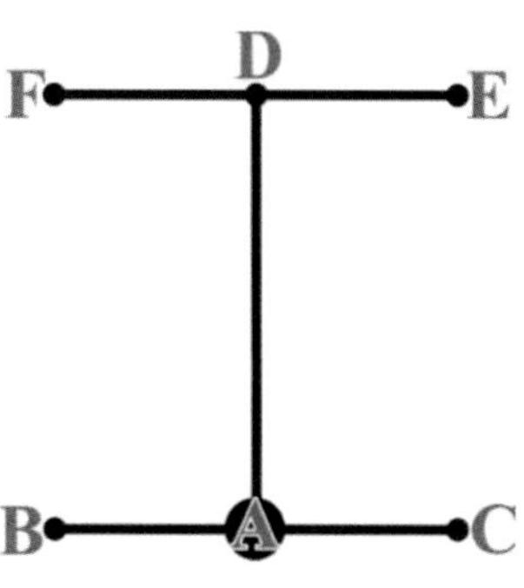


17: Bring left foot to right foot forming a **closed stance** (moa sogi) with your body facing **A** and your head turned toward **E**. Execute a left **high section downward hammerfist strike** (sahngdan naeryo meh joomok darigi).

18: Step right 90-degrees toward **F**, forming a **right foot forward front stance** (orun bal ahp sogi) and executing a right **middle section augmented forearm block** (chungdan kodoro makgi).

19: Maintain stance and execute a left **reverse high section spearhand (**sahngdan bahndae sohn-gut chirugi) with your palm downward.

20: Bring right foot to left foot forming a **closed stance** (moa sogi) with your body facing **A** and your head turned toward **F**. Execute a right **high section downward hammerfist strike** (sahngdan naeryo meh joomok darigi).

21: Step forward toward **A** with your right foot, forming a **right foot forward front stance** (orun bal ahp sogi) and executing a **low section X-forearm block** (hadan kyocha palmok makgi).

21, Alternate View

22: Step forward with the left foot onto line **AD** and form a **horse stance** (kima sogi). Execute a left **outer forearm block** (pakat palmok makgi).

22, Alternate View

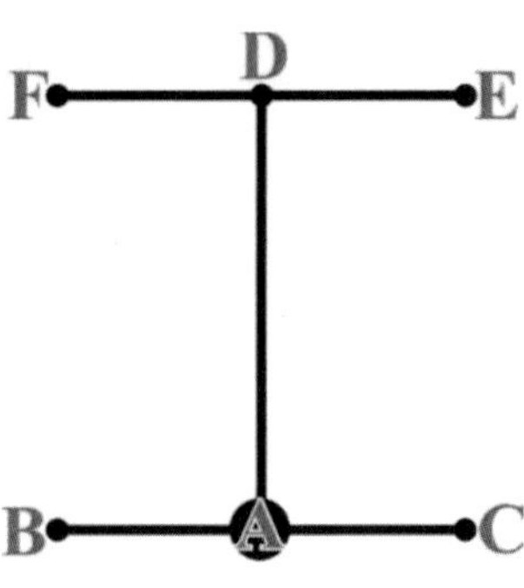

23: Execute a left leg **step behind side thrust kick** (bal-diro omgyo yup chagi) toward **A**.

23, Continued

23, Continued

24: Land in a **horse stance** (kima sogi) and execute a left **middle section augmented side elbow strike** (chungdan yup palkumchi darigi) toward **A**.

24, Alternate View

25: Step right foot past left foot, pivot 90-degrees so that you are facing **D** and shift your left foot into a **parallel stance** (narani sogi) while executing a **major hip throw** (o-goshi) over your left hip. **Kihap.**

25, Alternate View

25, Continued

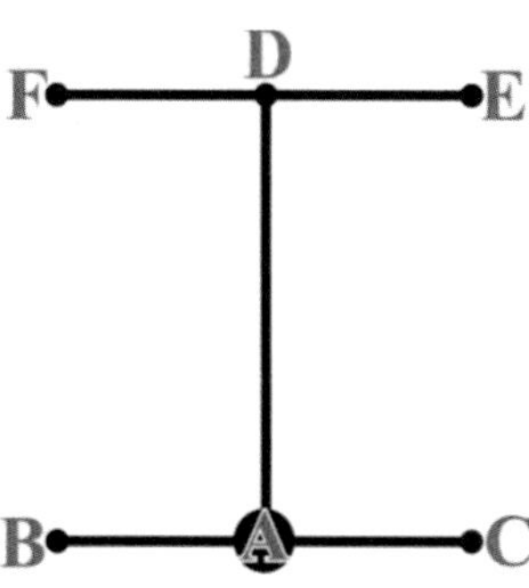

25, Continued, Alternate View

25, Continued

25, Continued, Alternate View

26: Pivot left foot 90-degrees toward **B** and form a **left foot forward back stance** (wen bal dwi sogi). Execute a left **deflection block** (bahn sah chakyong makgi).

26, Continued

27: Execute a right leg **roundhouse kick** (tollyo chagi) toward **B**.

27, Continued

28: Land forming a **right foot forward front stance** (orun bal ahp sogi). Execute a right **middle section forearm block** (chungdan palmok makgi).

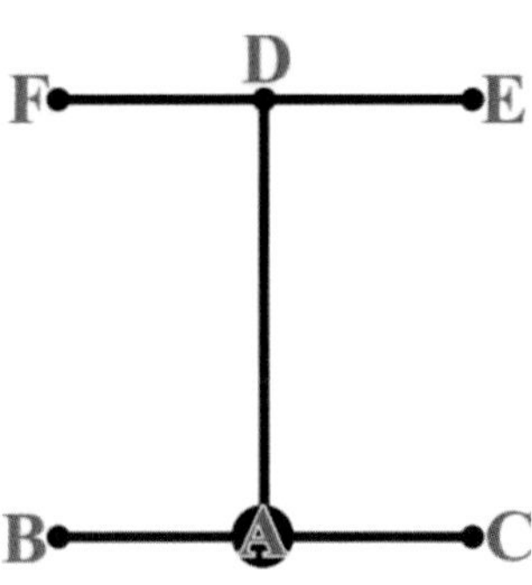

29: Maintain stance. Execute a left **reverse high section arc hand strike** (sahngdan bahndae bandal sohn chirugi).

30: Pivot clockwise 180-degrees toward **C** and form a **right foot forward back stance** (orun bal dwi sogi). Execute a right **deflection block** (bahn sah chakyong makgi).

30, Continued

30, Continued

31: Execute a left leg **roundhouse kick** (tollyo chagi) toward **C**.

31, Continued

32: Land forming a **left foot forward front stance** (wen bal ahp sogi). Execute a left **middle section forearm block** (chungdan palmok makgi).

33: Maintain stance. Execute a right **reverse high section arc hand strike** (sahngdan bahndae bandal sohn chirugi). **Kihap**.

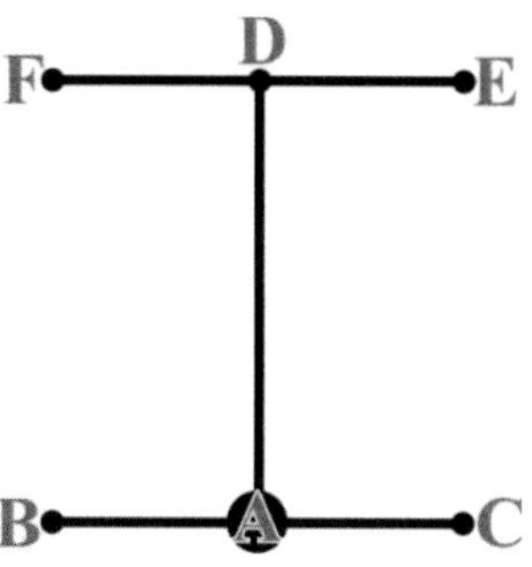

***Paro:*** Return Left Leg to Ready Position

Students testing for brown stripe must know form Chon Ji In Il Chang.

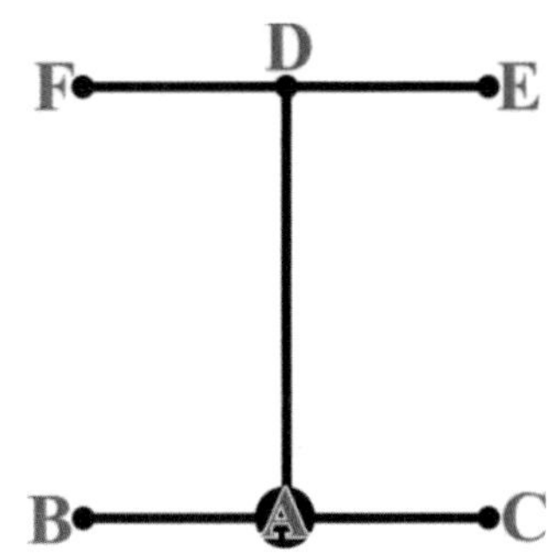


**Chon Ji In Il Chang: Sky.** The limitless potential for the development and well-being of the individual.

**Ready Position:** Parallel stance pushing high section double arc hand at A facing D.

**Movements:**

1: Step left foot 90-degrees toward **B** forming a **left foot forward back stance** (wen bal dwi sogi). Execute a left **middle section corkscrew trap, in to out** (kamuh toe olgami) taking care that the circle is large enough to trap an opponent's arm. **Kihap**.

2: Maintain trap and shift left foot, forming a **left foot forward front stance** (wen bal ahp sogi) facing **B**. Execute a right **reverse high section palm heel strike** (sahngdan bahndae sohn-bahdahk chirugi).

3: Maintain stance and execute a right **reverse low section palm heel strike** (hadan bahndae sohn-bahdahk chirugi) to the groin.

4: Shift from a left foot forward front stance to a **left foot forward back stance** (wen bal dwi sogi). Simultaneously execute a left **middle section palm heel pushing block** (chungdan sohn-bahdahk miro makgi) while bringing right fist up to guard the side of your face (olgool makgi).

5: Step forward toward **B** forming a **right foot forward front stance** (orun bal ahp sogi) and execute a right **middle section front punch** (chungdan ahp joomok chirugi).

6: Turn clockwise 180-degrees toward **C** forming a **right foot forward back stance** (orun bal dwi sogi). Execute a right **middle section corkscrew trap, in to out** (kamuh toe olgami) taking care that the circle is large enough to trap an opponent's arm.

7: Maintain trap and shift right foot, forming a **right foot forward front stance** (orun bal ahp sogi) facing **C**. Execute a left **reverse high section palm heel strike** (sahngdan bahndae sohn-bahdahk chirugi).

8: Maintain stance and execute a left **reverse low section palm heel strike** (hadan bahndae sohn-bahdahk chirugi) to the groin.

9: Shift from a right foot forward front stance to a **right foot forward back stance** (orun bal dwi sogi). Simultaneously execute a right **middle section palm heel pushing block** (chungdan sohn-bahdahk miro makgi) while bringing left fist up to guard the side of your face (olgool makgi).

10: Step forward toward **C** forming a **left foot forward front stance** (wen bal ahp sogi) and execute a left **middle section front punch** (chungdan ahp joomok chirugi).

11: Step left foot 90-degrees toward **D** to form a **left foot forward front stance** (wen bal ahp sogi) and execute a **low section X-forearm block** (hadan kyocha palmok makgi).

12: Step forward with the right foot onto line **AD** and form a **horse stance** (kima sogi). Execute a right **outer forearm block** (pakat palmok makgi).

13: Execute a right leg **step behind side thrust kick** (bal-diro omgyo yup chagi) toward **D**.

14: Land in a **horse stance** (kima sogi) and execute a right **middle section augmented side elbow strike** (chungdan yup palkumchi churigi) toward **D**. **Kihap**.

15: Pivot counterclockwise with your left foot toward **E**, forming a **left foot forward front stance** (wen bal ahp sogi) and executing a left **middle section augmented forearm block** (chungdan kodoro makgi).

16: Maintain stance and execute a right **reverse high section spearhand strike** (sahngdan bahndae sohn-gut chirugi) with your palm downward.

17: Bring left foot to right foot forming a **closed stance** (moa sogi) with your body facing **A** and your head turned toward **E**. Execute a left **high section downward hammerfist strike** (sahngdan naeryo meh joomok darigi).

18: Step right 90-degrees toward **F**, forming a **right foot forward front stance** (orun bal ahp sogi) and executing a right **middle section augmented forearm block** (chungdan kodoro makgi).

19: Maintain stance and execute a left **reverse high section spearhand strike** (sahngdan bahndae sohn-gut chirugi) with your palm downward.

20: Bring right foot to left foot forming a **closed stance** (moa sogi) with your body facing **A** and your head turned toward **F**. Execute a right **high section downward hammerfist strike** (sahngdan naeryo meh joomok darigi).

21: Step forward toward **A** with your right foot, forming a **right foot forward front stance** (orun bal ahp sogi) and executing a **low section X-forearm block** (hadan kyocha palmok makgi).

22: Step forward with the left foot onto line **AD** and form a **horse stance** (kima sogi). Execute a left **outer forearm block** (pakat palmok makgi).

23: Execute a left leg **step behind side thrust kick** (bal-diro omgyo yup chagi) toward **A**.

24: Land in a **horse stance** (kima sogi) and execute a left **middle section augmented side elbow strike** (chungdan yup palkumchi darigi) toward **A**.

25: Step right foot past left foot, pivot 90-degrees so that you are facing **D** and shift your left foot into a **parallel stance** (narani sogi) while executing a **major hip throw** (o-goshi) over your left hip. **Kihap.**

26: Pivot left foot 90-degrees toward **B** and form a **left foot forward back stance** (wen bal dwi sogi). Execute a left **deflection block** (bahn sah chakyong makgi).

27: Execute a right leg **roundhouse kick** (tollyo chagi) toward **B**.

28: Land forming a **right foot forward front stance** (orun bal ahp sogi). Execute a right **middle section forearm block** (chungdan palmok makgi).

29: Maintain stance. Execute a left **reverse high section arc hand strike** (sahngdan bahndae bandal sohn chirugi).

30: Pivot clockwise 180-degrees toward **C** and form a **right foot forward back stance** (orun bal dwi sogi). Execute a right **deflection block** (bahn sah chakyong makgi).

31: Execute a left leg **roundhouse kick** (tollyo chagi) toward **C**.

32: Land forming a **left foot forward front stance** (wen bal ahp sogi). Execute a left **middle section forearm block** (chungdan palmok makgi).

33: Maintain stance. Execute a right **reverse high section arc hand strike** (sahngdan bahndae bandal sohn chirugi). **Kihap**.

***Paro:*** Return Left Leg to Ready Position.

# 천지인이장

# Chonji In Yee Chang

(33 Movements)
Presented by Master Rick Steinmaier

**Chon Ji In Yee Chang:** **Earth.** Which has served as the one constant for the development of humanity.

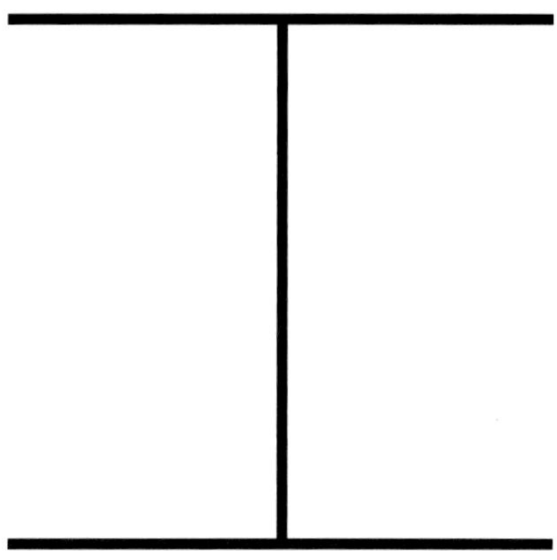

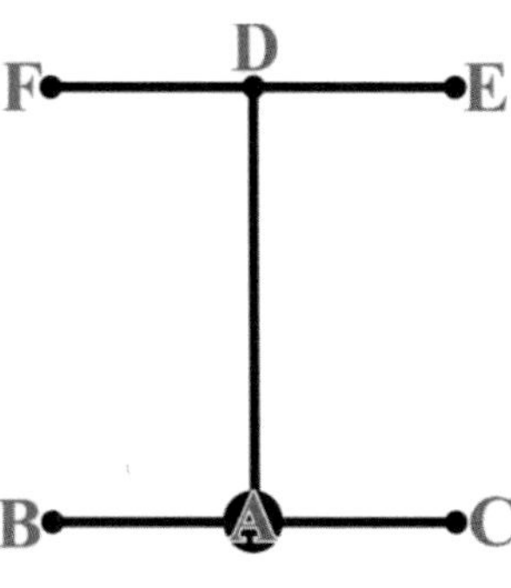


**Ready Position:** Parallel Stance Pushing Low Section Double Arc Hand.

1: Move left foot to form a **horse stance** (kima sogi) on line **AB**, facing forward. Execute a right **high section augmented rolling vertical punch** (sahngdan sewo joomok chirugi) with the left hand under the right elbow. **Kihap**.

1, Continued

2: Shift left foot 90-degrees toward **B** forming a **left foot forward back stance** (wen bal dwi sogi) and execute a left **middle section outward ridgehand block** (chungdan bakuro yuk sohn-kal makgi).

3: Step forward toward **B** forming a **right foot forward front stance** (orun bal ahp sogi) and execute a right **low section palm heel strike** (hadan sohn-bahdahk chirugi) to the groin.

4: Pivot 180-degrees clockwise toward **A**, forming a **right foot forward back stance** (orun bal dwi sogi) and execute a right **middle section outward ridgehand block** (chungdan bakuro yuk sohn-kal makgi).

5: Step forward toward **C** forming a **left foot forward front stance** (wen bal ahp sogi) and execute a left **low section palm heel strike** (hadan sohn-bahdahk chirugi) to the groin.

6: Step 90-degrees toward **D** with the left foot, forming a **left foot forward front stance** (wen bal ahp sogi) and execute a left **low section knifehand block** (hadan sohn-kal makgi).

6, Continued

7: Maintain stance. Pull both hands to right side in a stacking chamber with left hand on top. Simultaneously execute a left **high section knifehand block** (sahngdan sohn-kal makgi) and a right **reverse high section inward knifehand strike** (sahngdan bahndae anuro sohn-kal darigi).

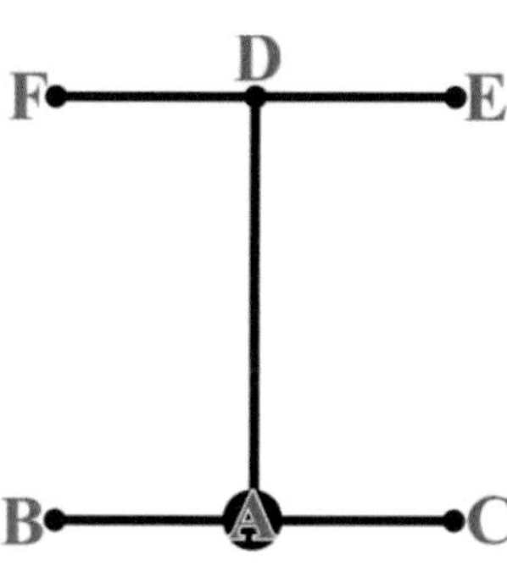


7, Continued

8: Move forward toward **D** executing a right leg **front snap kick** (ahp chagi).

8, Continued

9: Land in a **right foot forward front stance** (orun bal ahp sogi), executing a right **middle section augmented vertical spearhand strike** (chungdan sewo sohn-gut chirugi).

10: Maintain stance. Execute a right **wrist grab escape** (sohn mok chopki pulgi).

10, Continued

11: Maintain stance. Execute a right **high section downward backfist strike** (sahngdan naeryo deung joomok darigi) with your knuckles facing forward.

12: Move forward executing a left leg **roundhouse kick** (tollyo chagi).

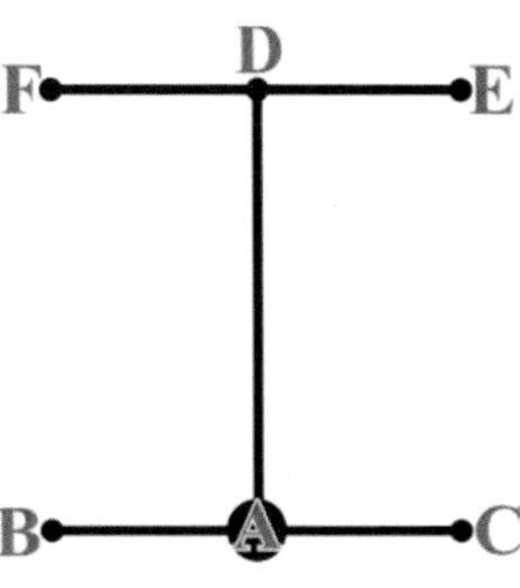

12, Continued

13: Land in a transitional stance. Move forward executing a right leg **roundhouse kick** (tollyo chagi).

13, Continued

14: Land forming a **right foot forward back stance** (orun bal dwi sogi), executing a **middle section double knifehand block** (chungdan dool sohn-kal makgi).

15: Move left leg 270-degrees counterclockwise, forming a **left foot forward back stance** (wen bal dwi sogi) facing **E**. Stack and execute a **knifehand box block** (sahng sohn sohn-kal makgi).

15, Continued

16: Step forward into a **right foot forward front stance** (orun bal ahp sogi), executing a right **middle section vertical punch** (chungdan sewo joomok chirugi). At the same time, execute a left hand **reverse palm heel face block** (bahndae sohn-bahdahk olgool makgi), bringing your left hand to the right side of your face.

17: Turn 180-degrees clockwise, forming a **right foot forward back stance** (orun bal dwi sogi) facing **F**. Stack and execute a **knifehand box block** (sahng sohn sohn-kal makgi).

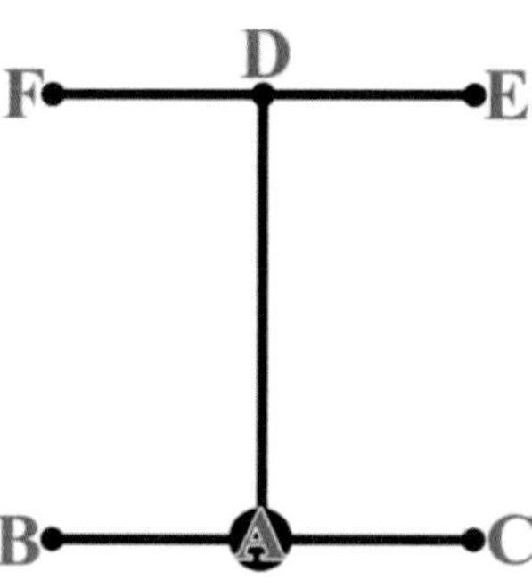

17, Continued

18: Step forward into a **left foot forward front stance** (wen bal ahp sogi), executing a left **middle section vertical punch** (chungdan sewo joomok chirugi). At the same time, execute a right hand **reverse palm heel face block** (bahndae sohn-bahdahk olgool makgi), bringing your right hand to the left side of your face.

19: Step 90-degrees toward **A** with the left foot, forming a **left foot forward front stance** (wen bal ahp sogi) and execute a left **low section knifehand block** (hadan sohn-kal makgi).

19, Continued

20: Maintain stance. Pull left hand to right side in a stacking chamber with left hand on top. Simultaneously execute a left **high section knifehand block** (sahngdan sohn-kal makgi) and a right **reverse high section inward knifehand strike** (sahngdan bahndae anuro sohn-kal darigi).

20, Continued

20, Continued, Alternate View

21: Move forward, executing a right leg **roundhouse kick** (tollyo chagi).

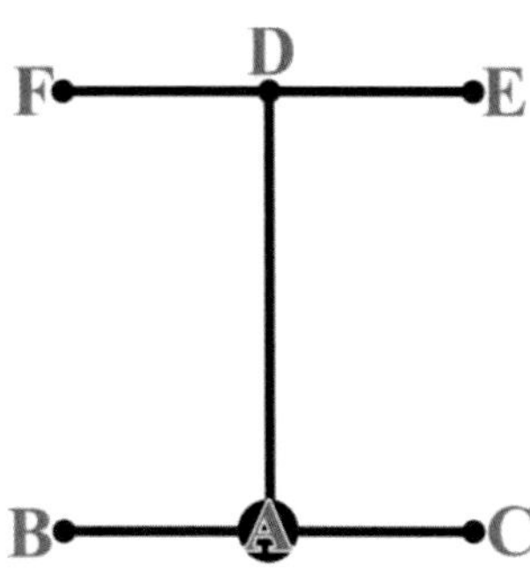

21, Continued

22: Land in a **right foot forward back stance** (orun bal dwi sogi) facing **A**. Execute a **middle section Kyuki-Do block** (chungdan Kyuki-Do makgi).

22, Alternate View (note position and orientation of back hand.)

23: Grab opponent's right arm and left lapel and move your left foot past your right foot, pivot 90-degrees and shift your right foot into a **parallel stance** (narani sogi) facing **D**. Execute a **two-handed shoulder throw** (morote seionage).

23, Continued

23, Continued

23, Continued

24: Step forward toward **D** into a **left foot forward front stance** (wen bal ahp sogi) and execute a right **reverse downward palm heel strike** (bahndae naeryo sohn-bahdahk chirugi). **Kihap**.

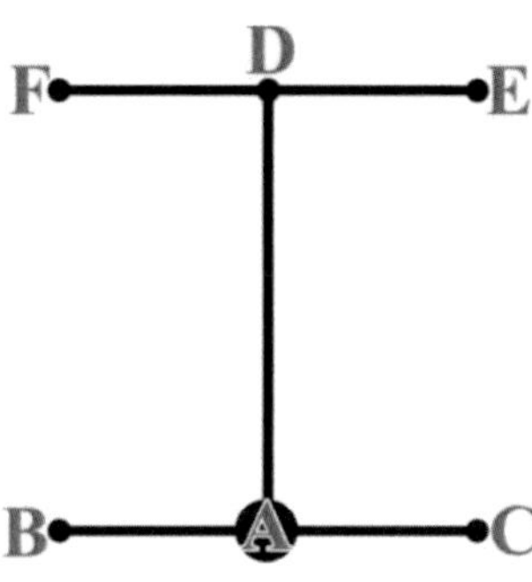

25: From your current stance, look 180-degrees over your left shoulder and execute a left leg **side thrust kick** (yup chagi) toward **A**.

25, Continued

25, Continued, Alternate View

26: Land forming a **left foot forward back stance** (wen bal dwi sogi) facing **A**. Execute a **middle section Kyuki-Do block** (chungdan Kyuki-Do makgi).

26, Alternate View

27: Grab opponent's right arm and step forward, bringing your right arm up under their right arm. Move your left foot past your right foot, pivot 90-degrees and shift your right foot into a **parallel stance** (narani sogi) facing **D**. Execute a **one-armed shoulder throw** (ippon seionage).

27, Continued

27, Continued

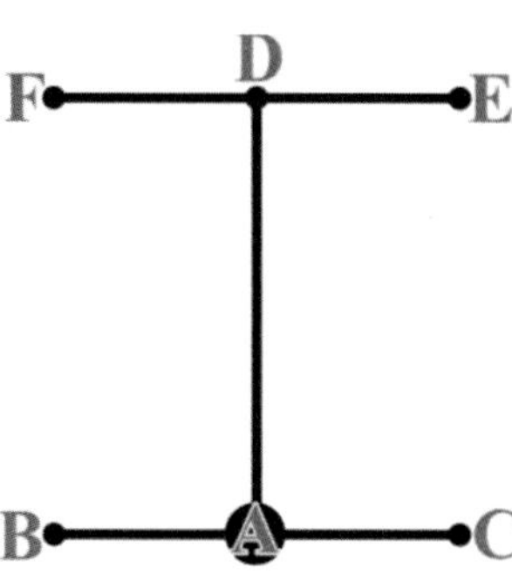

27, Continued

28: Straighten up and execute a right foot **stomping kick** (pahlba chagi). Return right foot to a **closed stance** (moa sogi). **Kihap**.

29: Look 180-degrees over left shoulder and execute a left leg **side thrust kick** (yup chagi) toward **A**.

29, Continued

29, Continued, Alternate View

30: Land forming a **left foot forward back stance** (wen bal dwi sogi) facing **A**. Execute a **middle section Kyuki-Do block** (chungdan Kyuki-Do makgi).

30, Alternate View

31: Pivot 180-degrees on left foot and execute a right **rear leg side thrust kick** (dwi bal yup chagi) toward **A**.

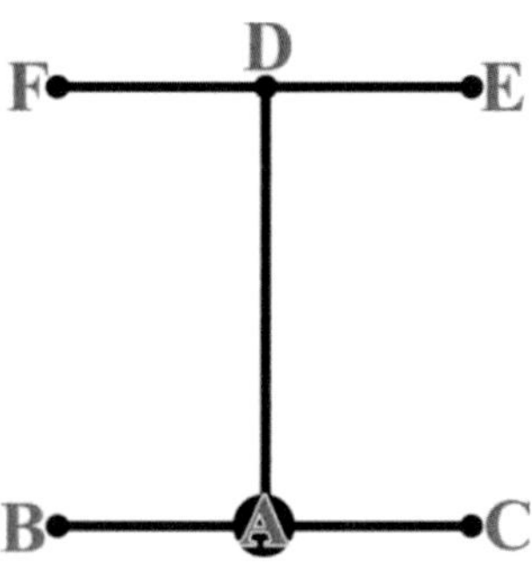

31, Continued

32: Land forming a **left leg forward cat stance** (wen bal goyangi sogi) at **A** facing **D**. Execute a right **reverse middle section vertical punch** (chungdan bahndae sewo joomok chirugi). At the same time, execute a left hand **palm heel face block** (sohn-bahdahk olgool makgi), bringing your left hand to the right side of your face.

33: Step forward with your left foot into a **left foot forward front stance** (wen bal ahp sogi) executing a right hand **reverse high section spearhand strike** (sahngdan bahndae sohn-gut chirugi). **Kihap**.

***Paro:*** Return Right Leg to Ready Position

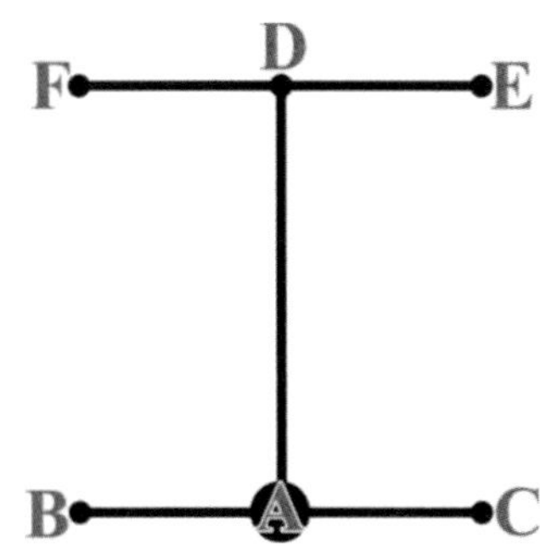


Students testing for brown belt must know form Chon Ji In Yee Chang.

**Chon Ji In Yee Chang: Earth.** Which has served as the one constant for the development of humanity.
**Ready Position:** Parallel stance pushing low section double arc hand at A facing D.
**Movements:**

1: Move left foot to form a **horse stance** (kima sogi) on line **AB**, facing forward. Execute a right **high section augmented rolling vertical punch** (sahngdan sewo joomok chirugi) with the left hand under the right elbow. **Kihap**.

2: Shift left foot 90-degrees toward **B** forming a **left foot forward back stance** (wen bal dwi sogi) and execute a left **middle section outward ridgehand block** (chungdan bakuro yuk sohn-kal makgi).

3: Step forward toward **B** forming a **right foot forward front stance** (orun bal ahp sogi) and execute a right **low section palm heel strike** (hadan sohn-bahdahk chirugi) to the groin.

4: Pivot 180-degrees clockwise toward **A**, forming a **right foot forward back stance** (orun bal dwi sogi) and execute a right **middle section outward ridgehand block** (chungdan bakuro yuk sohn-kal makgi).

5: Step forward toward **C** forming a **left foot forward front stance** (wen bal ahp sogi) and execute a left **low section palm heel strike** (hadan sohn-bahdahk chirugi) to the groin.

6: Step 90-degrees toward **D** with the left foot, forming a **left foot forward front stance** (wen bal ahp sogi) and execute a left **low section knifehand block** (hadan sohn-kal makgi).

7: Maintain stance. Pull both hands to right side in a stacking chamber with left hand on top. Simultaneously execute a left **high section knifehand block** (sahngdan sohn-kal makgi) and a right **reverse high section inward knifehand strike** (sahngdan bahndae anuro sohn-kal darigi).

8: Move forward toward **D** executing a right leg **front snap kick** (ahp chagi).

9: Land in a **right foot forward front stance** (orun bal ahp sogi), executing a right **middle section augmented vertical spearhand strike** (chungdan sewo Sohn-gut chirugi).

10: Maintain stance. Execute a right **wrist grab escape** (sohn mok chopki pulgi).

11: Maintain stance. Execute a right **high section downward backfist strike** (sahngdan naeryo deung joomok darigi) with your knuckles facing forward.

12: Move forward executing a left leg **roundhouse kick** (tollyo chagi).

13: Land in a transitional stance. Move forward executing a right leg **roundhouse kick** (tollyo chagi).

14: Land forming a **right foot forward back stance** (orun bal dwi sogi), executing a **middle section double knifehand block** (chungdan dool sohn-kal makgi).

15: Move left leg 270-degrees counterclockwise, forming a **left foot forward back stance** (wen bal dwi sogi) facing **E**. Stack and execute a **knifehand box block** (sahng sohn sohn-kal makgi).

16: Step forward into a **right foot forward front stance** (orun bal ahp sogi), executing a right **middle section vertical punch** (chungdan sewo joomok chirugi). At the same time, execute a left hand **reverse palm heel face block** (bahndae sohn-bahdahk olgool makgi), bringing your left hand to the right side of your face.

17: Turn 180-degrees clockwise, forming a **right foot forward back stance** (orun bal dwi sogi) facing **F**. Stack and execute a **knifehand box block** (sahng sohn sohn-kal makgi).

18: Step forward into a **left foot forward front stance** (wen bal ahp sogi), executing a left **middle section vertical punch** (chungdan sewo joomok chirugi). At the same time, execute a right hand **reverse palm heel face block** (bahndae sohn-bahdahk olgool makgi), bringing your right hand to the left side of your face.

19: Step 90-degrees toward **A** with the left foot, forming a **left foot forward front stance** (wen bal ahp sogi) and execute a left **low section knifehand block** (hadan sohn-kal makgi).

20: Maintain stance. Pull left hand to right side in a stacking chamber with left hand on top. Simultaneously execute a left **high section knifehand block** (sahngdan sohn-kal makgi) and a right **reverse high section inward knifehand strike** (sahngdan bahndae anuro sohn-kal darigi).

21: Move forward, executing a right leg **roundhouse kick** (tollyo chagi).

22: Land in a **right foot forward back stance** (orun bal dwi sogi) facing **A**. Execute a **middle section Kyuki-Do block** (chungdan Kyuki-Do makgi).

23: Grab opponent's right arm and left lapel and move your left foot past your right foot, pivot 90-degrees and shift your right foot into a **parallel stance** (narani sogi) facing **D**. Execute a **two-handed shoulder throw** (morote seionage).

24: Step forward toward **D** into a **left foot forward front stance** (wen bal ahp sogi) and execute a right **reverse downward palm heel strike** (bahndae naeryo sohn-bahdahk chirugi). **Kihap**.

25: From your current stance, look 180-degrees over your left shoulder and execute a left leg **side thrust kick** (yup chagi) toward **A**.

26: Land forming a **left foot forward back stance** (wen bal dwi sogi) facing **A**. Execute a **middle section Kyuki-Do block** (chungdan Kyuki-Do makgi).

27: Grab opponent's right arm and step forward, bringing your right arm up under their right arm. Move your left foot past your right foot, pivot 90-degrees and shift your right foot into a **parallel stance** (narani sogi) facing **D**. Execute a **one-armed shoulder throw** (ippon seionage).

28: Straighten up and execute a right foot **stomping kick** (pahlba chagi). Return right foot to a **closed stance** (moa sogi). **Kihap**.

29: Look 180-degrees over left shoulder and execute a left leg **side thrust kick** (yup chagi) toward **A**.

30: Land forming a **left foot forward back stance** (wen bal dwi sogi) facing **A**. Execute a **middle section Kyuki-Do block** (chungdan Kyuki-Do makgi).

31: Pivot 180 degrees on left foot and execute a right **rear leg side thrust kick** (dwi bal yup chagi) toward **A**.

32: Land forming a **left leg forward cat stance** (wen bal goyangi sogi) at **A** facing **D**. Execute a right **reverse middle section vertical punch** (chungdan bahndae sewo joomok chirugi). At the same time, execute a left hand **palm heel face block** (sohn-bahdahk olgool makgi), bringing your left hand to the right side of your face.

33: Step forward with your left foot into a **left foot forward front stance** (wen bal ahp sogi) executing a right hand **reverse high section spearhand strike** (sahngdan bahndae sohn-gut chirugi). **Kihap**.

***Paro:*** Return Right Leg to Ready Position

# 천지인삼장

# CHONJI IN SAM CHANG

(33 Movements)
Presented by Master Ken Blumreich

**Chon Ji In Sam Chang:** **People.** Humankind, which fills the cosmos with hopes, dreams and the uniqueness within each person; which together with the earth and heaven makes up the universe in which we live.

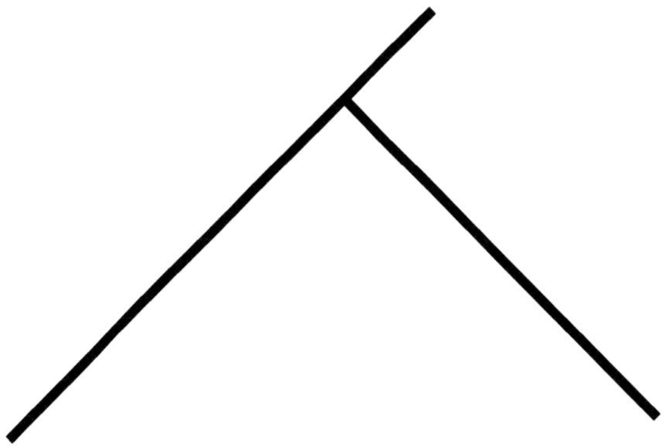

**Ready Position:** Parallel Stance Pushing Middle Section Double Arc Hand.

1: Step left foot toward **B**, forming a **left classical Kyuki-Do stance** (wen bal Kyuki-Do sogi) with your feet along line **AB**. Look back over your right shoulder toward **A** and execute a **modified Kyuki-Do block** (byun gyun Kyuki-Do maki). **Kihap.**

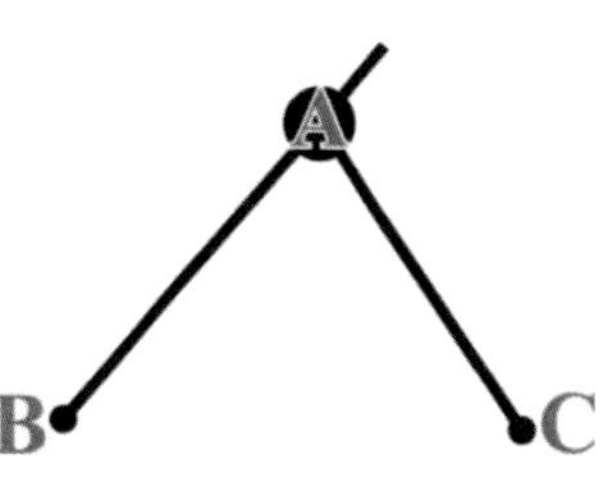

2: Jump forward, bringing left foot toward right foot. Execute a right leg **connecting side thrust kick** (eeh oh yup chagi) away from **B**.

3: Land in a **left foot forward back stance** (wen bal dwi sogi) facing **B**. Execute a **middle section double knifehand block** (chungdan dool sohn-kal makgi).

4: Note: The following three movements are executed in quick succession. Step forward toward **B** into a transitional stance, executing a right hand **high section inward knifehand strike** (sahngdan anuro sohn-kal darigi).

5: Pivot counterclockwise on right foot, bringing left foot around 180 degrees into a transitional stance facing **B** while executing a **high section outward knifehand strike** (sahngdan bakuro sohn-kal darigi).

5, Continued

5, Continued

6: Step forward into a **right foot forward front stance** (orun bal ahp sogi) facing **B** while executing a right hand **high section inward knifehand strike** (sahngdan anuro sohn-kal darigi).

7: Execute a right **connecting front snap kick** (eeh oh ahp chagi) toward **B**.

7, Continued

7, Continued

8: Land in a **right foot forward front stance** (orun bal ahp sogi) and execute a high section **normal cross choke** (nami juje jime) with right hand over left. Bend left knee and shift backwards while bringing your hands to your chest to complete the choke.

8, Continued

8, Continued, Alternate View (note that right hand is on top of left.)

9: Straighten your left knee and shift forward in a **right foot forward front stance** (orun bal ahp sogi). Execute a right hand **high section knifehand block** (sahngdan sohn-kal makgi), catching opponent under the chin and snapping their head up and back.

10: Maintain stance and execute a left hand **reverse high section arc hand strike** (sahngdan bahndae bandal sohn chirugi).

11: Pivot on right foot and execute a left **roundhouse kick** (tollyo chagi) toward **B**.

12: Land in a transitional stance and execute a 180-degree **spinning hook kick** (dwi tollyo golcha chagi) toward **B**.

12, Continued

13: Land in a **left foot forward back stance** (wen bal dwi sogi) at **B** facing **A**. Execute a **guarding block** (daebi makgi).

13, Continued

14: Jump forward and land in an **X-stance** (kyocha sogi) with your left foot behind your right foot while executing a **high section vertical backfist strike** (sahngdan sewo deung joomok darigi).

14, Continued

14, Continued

15: Pivot counterclockwise 180 degrees, unwinding into a **left foot forward back stance** (wen bal dwi sogi) with a **high section outward knifehand strike** (sahngdan bakuro sohn-kal darigi).

15, Continued

16: Step forward toward **A** forming a **right foot forward front stance** (orun bal ahp sogi). Execute a right **middle section front punch** (chungdan ahp joomok chirugi).

17: Step forward toward **A** forming a **left foot forward front stance** (wen bal ahp sogi), executing a **middle section twin palm heel strike** (chungdan sahng sohn-bahdahk chirugi). **Kihap**.

18: Move left foot, forming a transitional **parallel stance** (narani sogi) along line **AB**. Execute a clockwise jump. Land in a **right foot forward back stance** (orun bal dwi sogi) facing **C**. Execute a **middle section double knifehand block** (chungdan dool sohn-kal makgi).

18, Continued

18, Continued

19: Note: The following three movements are executed in quick succession. Step forward toward **C** into a transitional stance, executing a left hand **high section inward knifehand strike** (sahngdan anuro sohn-kal darigi).

20: Pivot counterclockwise on left foot, bringing right foot around 180 degrees into a transitional stance facing **C** while executing a **high section outward knifehand strike** (sahngdan bakuro sohn-kal darigi).

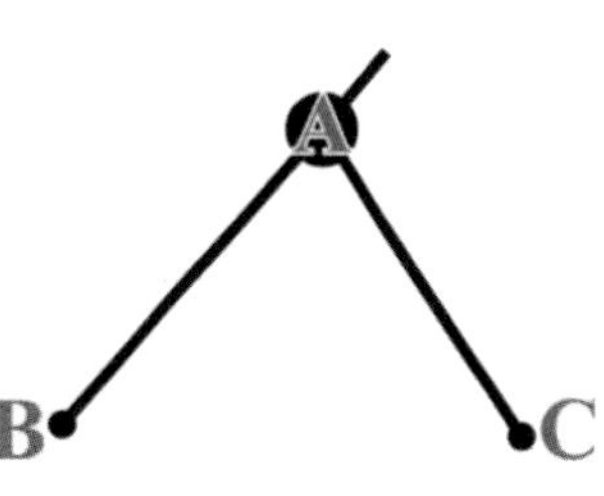

20, Continued

20, Continued

21: Step forward into a **left foot forward front stance** (wen bal ahp sogi) facing **C** while executing a left hand **high section inward knifehand strike** (sahngdan anuro sohn-kal darigi).

22: Execute a left **connecting front snap kick** (eeh oh ahp chagi) toward **C**.

22, Continued

22, Continued

23: Land in a **left foot forward front stance** (wen bal ahp sogi) and execute a high section **normal cross choke** (nami juje jime) with left hand over right. Bend right knee and shift backwards while bringing your hands to your chest to complete the choke.

23, Continued

23, Continued, Alternate View (note that left hand is on top of right.)

24: Straighten your right knee and shift forward in a **left foot forward front stance** (wen bal ahp sogi) again. Execute a left hand **high section knifehand block** (sahngdan sohn-kal makgi), catching opponent under the chin and snapping their head up and back.

25: Maintain stance and execute a right hand **reverse high section arc hand strike** (sahngdan bahndae bandal sohn chirugi).

26: Pivot on left foot and execute a right **roundhouse kick** (tollyo chagi) toward **C**.

27: Land in a transitional stance and execute a 180-degree **spinning hook kick** (dwi tollyo golcha chagi) toward **C**.

27, Continued

28: Land in a **right foot forward back stance** (orun bal dwi sogi) at **C** facing **A**. Execute a **guarding block** (daebi makgi).

28, Continued

29: Jump forward and land in an **X-stance** (kyocha sogi) with your right foot behind your left foot while executing a **high section vertical backfist strike** (sahngdan sewo deung joomok darigi).

29, Continued

29, Continued

30: Pivot clockwise 180 degrees, unwinding into a **right foot forward back stance** (orun bal dwi sogi) with a **high section outward knifehand strike** (sahngdan bakuro sohn-kal darigi).

30, Continued

31: Step forward toward **A** forming a **left foot forward front stance** (wen bal ahp sogi). Execute a left **middle section front punch** (chungdan ahp joomok chirugi).

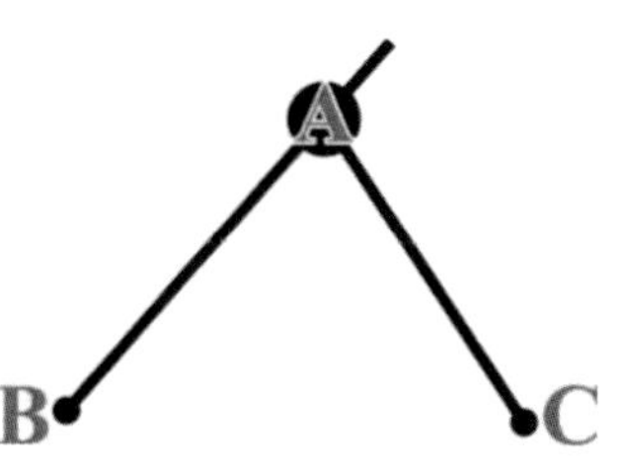


32: Step backward with your left leg, forming a **right foot forward kneeling front stance** (orun bal murrup gurro sogi). Execute a right **middle section knifehand block** (chungdan sohn-kal makgi).

33: Execute a right **forward roll** (zenpo kaiten) toward **A**. Land at **A** in a **right foot forward kneeling front stance** (orun bal murrup gurro sogi). As you come out of the roll, execute a right **high section knifehand block** (sahngdan sohn-kal makgi) and a left **reverse upwards ridgehand strike** (bahndae wi yuk sohn-kal darigi) to opponent's groin. **Kihap**.

33, Continued

33, Continued

***Paro:*** Return Left Foot to Ready Position.

Students testing for red stripe must know form Chon Ji In Sam Chang.

**Chon Ji In Sam Chang: People.** Humankind, which fills the cosmos with hopes, dreams and the uniqueness within each person; which together with the earth and heaven makes up the universe in which we live.

**Ready Position:** Parallel stance pushing middle section double arc hand at A facing forward.

**Movements:**

1: Step left foot toward **B**, forming a **left classical Kyuki-Do stance** (wen bal Kyuki-Do sogi) with your feet along line **AB**. Look back over your right shoulder toward **A** and execute a **modified Kyuki-Do block** (byun gyun Kyuki-Do maki). **Kihap.**

2: Jump forward, bringing left foot toward right foot. Execute a right leg **connecting side thrust kick** (eeh oh yup chagi) away from **B**.

3: Land in a **left foot forward back stance** (wen bal dwi sogi) facing **B**. Execute a **middle section double knifehand block** (chungdan dool sohn-kal makgi).

4: Note: The following three movements are executed in quick succession. Step forward toward **B** into a transitional stance, executing a right hand **high section inward knifehand strike** (sahngdan anuro sohn-kal darigi).

5: Pivot counterclockwise on right foot, bringing left foot around 180 degrees into a transitional stance facing **B** while executing a **high section outward knifehand strike** (sahngdan bakuro sohn-kal darigi).

6: Step forward into a **right foot forward front stance** (orun bal ahp sogi) facing **B** while executing a right hand **high section inward knifehand strike** (sahngdan anuro sohn-kal darigi).

7: Execute a right **connecting front snap kick** (eeh oh ahp chagi) toward **B**.

8: Land in a **right foot forward front stance** (orun bal ahp sogi) and execute a high section **normal cross choke** (nami juje jime) with right hand over left. Bend left knee and shift backwards while bringing your hands to your chest to complete the choke.

9: Straighten your left knee and shift forward in a **right foot forward front stance** (orun bal ahp sogi). Execute a right hand **high section knifehand block** (sahngdan sohn-kal makgi), catching opponent under the chin and snapping their head up and back.

10: Maintain stance and execute a left hand **reverse high section arc hand strike** (sahngdan bahndae bandal sohn chirugi).

11: Pivot on right foot and execute a left **roundhouse kick** (tollyo chagi) toward **B**.

12: Land in a transitional stance and execute a 180-degree **spinning hook kick** (dwi tollyo golcha chagi) toward **B**.

13: Land in a **left foot forward back stance** (wen bal dwi sogi) at **B** facing **A**. Execute a **guarding block** (daebi makgi).

14: Jump forward and land in an **X-stance** (kyocha sogi) with your left foot behind your right foot while executing a **high section vertical backfist strike** (sahngdan sewo deung joomok darigi).

15: Pivot counterclockwise 180 degrees, unwinding into a **left foot forward back stance** (wen bal dwi sogi) with a **high section outward knifehand strike** (sahngdan bakuro sohn-kal darigi).

16: Step forward toward **A** forming a **right foot forward front stance** (orun bal ahp sogi). Execute a right **middle section front punch** (chungdan ahp joomok chirugi).

17: Step forward toward **A** forming a **left foot forward front stance** (wen bal ahp sogi), executing a **middle section twin palm heel strike** (chungdan sahng sohn-bahdahk chirugi). **Kihap**.

18: Move left foot, forming a transitional **parallel stance** (narani sogi) along line **AB**. Execute a clockwise jump. Land in a **right foot forward back stance** (orun bal dwi sogi) facing **C**. Execute a **middle section double knifehand block** (chungdan dool sohn-kal makgi).

19: Note: The following three movements are executed in quick succession. Step forward toward **C** into a transitional stance, executing a left hand **high section inward knifehand strike** (sahngdan anuro sohn-kal darigi).

20: Pivot counterclockwise on left foot, bringing right foot around 180 degrees into a transitional stance facing **C** while executing a **high section outward knifehand strike** (sahngdan bakuro sohn-kal darigi).

21: Step forward into a **left foot forward front stance** (wen bal ahp sogi) facing **C** while executing a left hand **high section inward knifehand strike** (sahngdan anuro sohn-kal darigi).

22: Execute a left **connecting front snap kick** (eeh oh ahp chagi) toward **C**.

23: Land in a **left foot forward front stance** (wen bal ahp sogi) and execute a high section **normal cross choke** (nami juje jime) with left hand over right. Bend right knee and shift backwards while bringing your hands to your chest to complete the choke.

24: Straighten your right knee and shift forward in a **left foot forward front stance** (wen bal ahp sogi) again. Execute a left hand **high section knifehand block** (sahngdan sohn-kal makgi), catching opponent under the chin and snapping their head up and back.

25: Maintain stance and execute a right hand **reverse high section arc hand strike** (sahngdan bahndae bandal sohn chirugi).

26: Pivot on left foot and execute a right **roundhouse kick** (tollyo chagi) toward **C**.

27: Land in a transitional stance and execute a 180-degree **spinning hook kick** (dwi tollyo golcha chagi) toward **C**.

28: Land in a **right foot forward back stance** (orun bal dwi sogi) at **C** facing **A**. Execute a **guarding block** (daebi makgi).

29: Jump forward and land in an **X-stance** (kyocha sogi) with your right foot behind your left foot while executing a **high section vertical backfist strike** (sahngdan sewo deung joomok darigi).

30: Pivot clockwise 180 degrees, unwinding into a **right foot forward back stance** (orun bal dwi sogi) with a **high section outward knifehand strike** (sahngdan bakuro sohn-kal darigi).

31: Step forward toward **A** forming a **left foot forward front stance** (wen bal ahp sogi). Execute a left **middle section front punch** (chungdan ahp joomok chirugi).

32: Step backward with your left leg, forming a **right foot forward kneeling front stance** (orun bal murrup gurro sogi). Execute a right **middle section knifehand block** (chungdan sohn-kal makgi).

33: Execute a right **forward roll** (zenpo kaiten) toward **A**. Land at **A** in a **right foot forward kneeling front stance** (orun bal murrup gurro sogi). As you come out of the roll, execute a right **high section knifehand block** (sahngdan sohn-kal makgi) and a left **reverse upwards ridgehand strike** (bahndae wi yuk sohn-kal darigi) to opponent's groin. **Kihap**.

***Paro:*** Return Left Foot to Ready Position.

# 만남

# Man Nam

(52 Movements)
Presented by Master Linda Imler

**Man Nam:** **Meet or Gather Together.** Learning from contact, we are the sum total of all the experiences we have had, represented by the coming together of the practitioner and the Bo staff.

**Ready Position:** Closed Ready Stance Staff to Right Side.

Bow, maintaining hand and weapon position

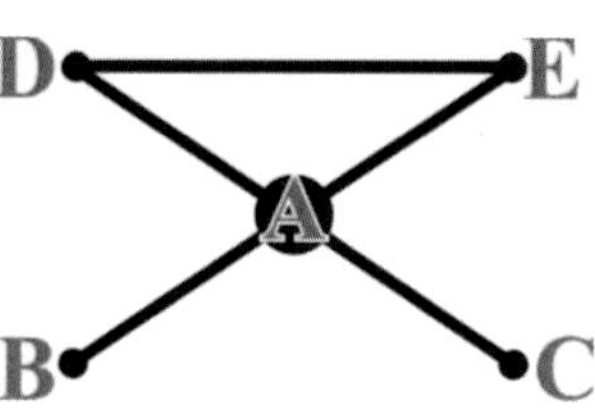

1: Step out with your left foot into a **parallel stance** (narani sogi) at **A**, facing the front of the room. Execute a **slow pushing twin high section horizontal block**. There is no **Kihap** on this move.

2: Maintain stance and execute a **twin low section horizontal block**.

2, Continued

3: Turn left toward **B** forming a **left foot forward front stance** (wen bal ahp sogi). As you are doing this, reverse your grip with your right hand and execute a **high section downward strike**. **Kihap**.

3, Continued

4: Shift your weight back, reset your grip with your right hand, forming a **left back stance** (wen bal dwi sogi) on line **AB** facing **B**. Execute a **classical box block**.

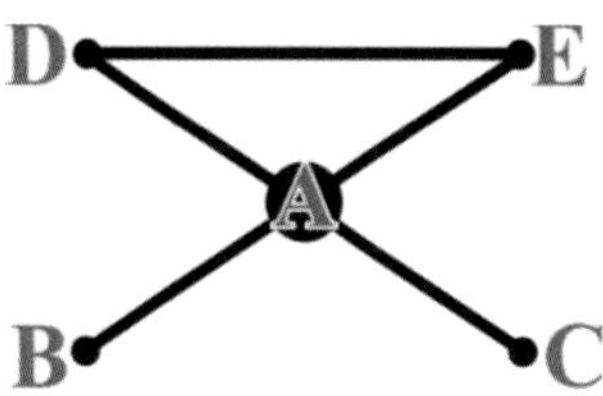


5: Bring your right foot forward into a transitional closed stance and let the staff drop to your right side. Step toward **B** with your left foot, forming a **left foot forward front stance** (wen bal ahp sogi). Execute a **reverse middle section poke**.

5, Continued

6: Note: the next three movements are done rapidly and illustrate **Body Conditioning**. Maintain stance. Execute a **low section strike**.

7: Maintain stance. Execute a **mid section strike**.

8: Maintain stance. Execute a **high section strike**.

9: Pivot on left foot and step right foot clockwise toward **A** and land in a **right foot forward front stance** (orun bal ahp sogi) along line **AB** facing **A**. Execute a **reverse middle section poke**.

10: Note: the next eight movements illustrate **Theory** and **Body Conditioning**. Step forward toward **E** into a **left foot forward front stance** (wen bal ahp sogi). Execute a **reverse middle section poke**.

11: Maintain stance and execute a **downward strike** toward the clavicle.

12: Maintain stance and execute a **reverse middle section poke**.

13: Maintain stance and execute an **upward strike** towards the groin.

14: Maintain stance and execute a **reverse middle section poke**.

15: Maintain stance and execute a **high section strike** (right to left), allowing the end of the staff to strike the outside of your arm.

16: Maintain stance and execute a **high section strike** (left to right), allowing the end of the staff to strike the outside of your arm.

17: Maintain stance and execute a **high section strike** (right to left), allowing the end of the staff to strike the outside of your arm.

18: Pivot on left foot and step right foot clockwise toward **C**, forming a **right foot forward front stance** (orun bal ahp sogi). As you are doing this, reverse your grip with your left hand and execute a **downward strike**. **Kihap**.

18, Continued

19: Shift your weight back and reset your grip with your left hand, forming a **right foot forward back stance** (orun bal dwi sogi) on line **AC** facing **C**. Execute a **classical box block**.

20: Bring your left foot forward into a transitional closed stance and let the staff drop to your left side. Step toward **C** with your right foot, forming a **right foot forward front stance** (orun bal ahp sogi). Execute a **reverse middle section poke**.

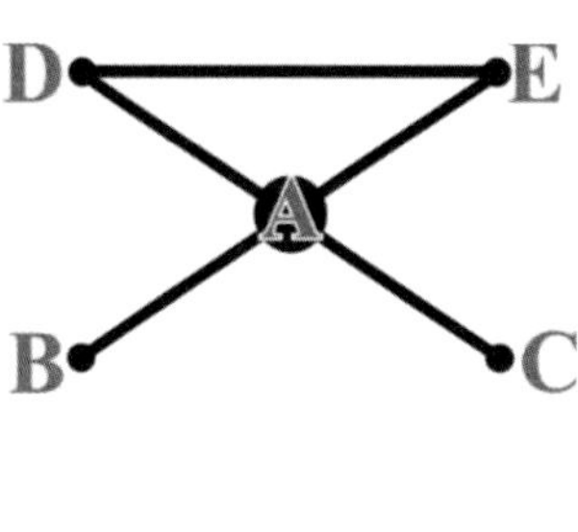

20, Continued

21: Note: the next three movements are done rapidly and illustrate **Body Conditioning**. Maintain stance. Execute a **low section strike**.

22: Maintain stance. Execute a **mid section strike**.

23: Maintain stance. Execute a **high section strike**.

24: Pivot on right foot and step left foot counterclockwise toward **A** and land in a **left foot forward front stance** (wen bal ahp sogi) along line **AC** facing **A**. Execute a **reverse middle section poke**.

25: Reverse grip with right hand and step forward toward **D**, forming a **right foot forward transitional stance**. Start executing a right hand **figure eight**. This is the first twirl.

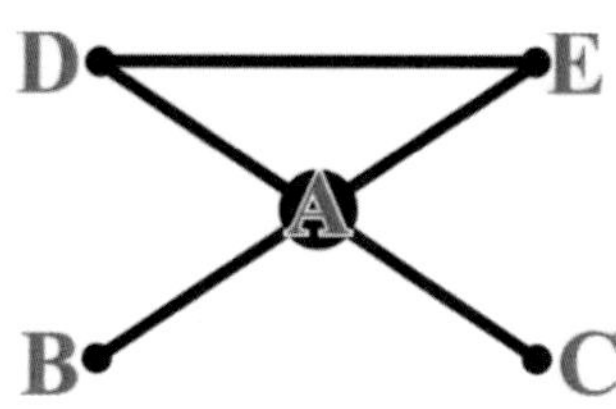

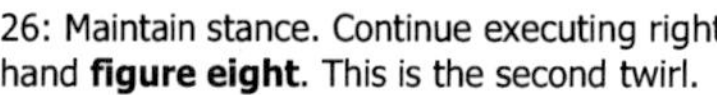
26: Maintain stance. Continue executing right hand **figure eight**. This is the second twirl.

  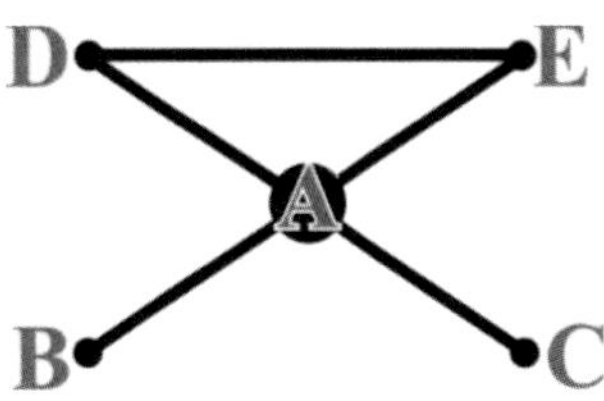

27: Maintain stance. Continue executing right hand **figure eight**. This is the third twirl.

28: Step forward toward **D**, forming a **left foot forward transitional stance**. Switch grip to left hand and begin executing a left hand **figure eight**. This is the first twirl.

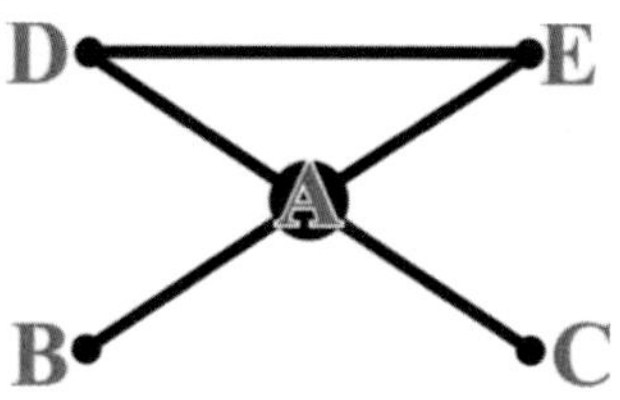

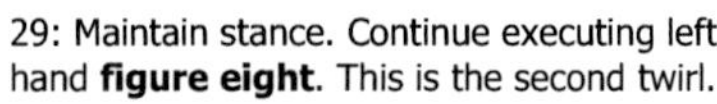

29: Maintain stance. Continue executing left hand **figure eight**. This is the second twirl.

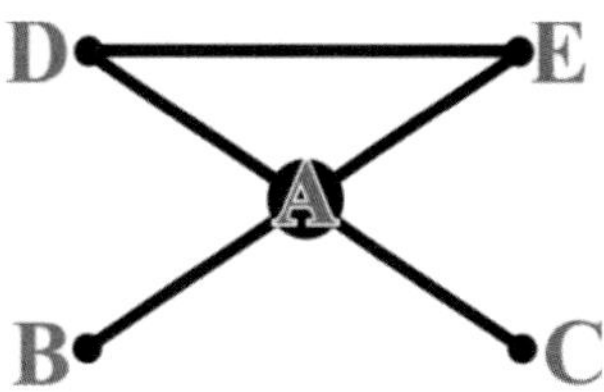


30: Maintain stance. Continue executing left hand **figure eight**. This is the third twirl.

31: Catch the staff on your right side, left hand palm up, right palm down. Reverse left grip and step forward into a **right foot forward front stance** (orun bal ahp sogi) executing a right **middle section poke**.

31, Continued

31, Continued

32: Step forward toward **D** into a **left foot forward front stance** (wen bal ahp sogi). Let go with your left hand and shift your left grip to the bottom of the staff. Execute an **overhead strike** down and to the left at a 45-degree angle. **Kihap**.

32, Continued

33: Draw right leg up into a **one legged stance** (han bal sogi). Execute a **high-low classical pose** with the bottom hand open.

34: Note: the next three moves are done together and illustrate **Manipulation**. Put your right foot down so that you are on line **DE** facing the front of the room. Slide your right hand to the center of the staff, palm inward. Turn your right hand clockwise, so that the palm faces away from you, causing the staff to spin 180-degrees.

34, Alternate View (Note that during sequence 34-36, the staff should be kept as close to parallel with the ground as possible.)

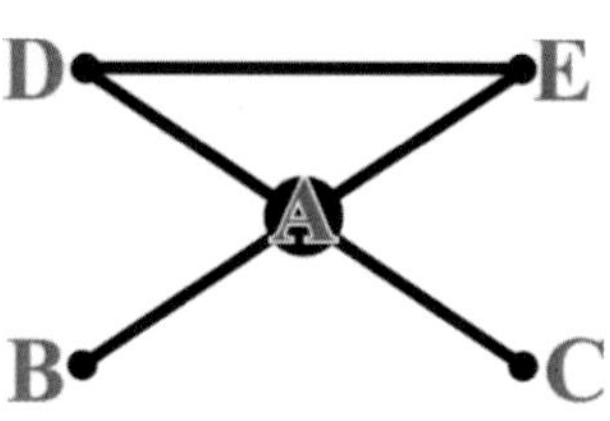

35: Step clockwise with your left foot landing in a transitional **horse stance** (kima sogi) along line **DE** facing the back of the room. As you step, bring the staff behind your back and switch from a right grip to a left grip.

35, Continued

35, Continued

35, Continued

36: Bring the staff back in front of you with your left hand facing palm out. Put the back of your right hand against the staff, with your palm facing toward you. Use your left hand to spin the staff clockwise into your right hand.

36, Continued

36, Continued: As you are doing this, step clockwise with your right foot ending up in a **right foot forward back stance** (orun bal dwi sogi) along line **DE**, facing **E**. While you are stepping, continue spinning the staff clockwise with your right hand.

36, Continued

36, Continued

36, Continued: At the end of the spin allow the end of the staff to strike you in the back while you execute a left hand **reverse high section knifehand block** (sahngdan bahndae sohn-kal makgi).

37: Step forward with your left foot into a **left foot forward front stance** (wen bal ahp sogi). Pass the staff over your right shoulder, from your right hand to your left hand.

38: Maintain stance. Execute a **reverse middle section poke**.

39: Maintain stance. Execute a **low section foot sweep**, using your right hand to drive the staff.

40: Maintain stance. Execute a **reverse high section strike**, ending with the staff tucked under your right arm.

41: Bring your right foot to your left foot, and execute a left leg **connecting front snap kick** (eeh oh ahp chagi). As you land, step toward **E** with your right foot, forming a transitional stance along line **DE**.

41, Continued

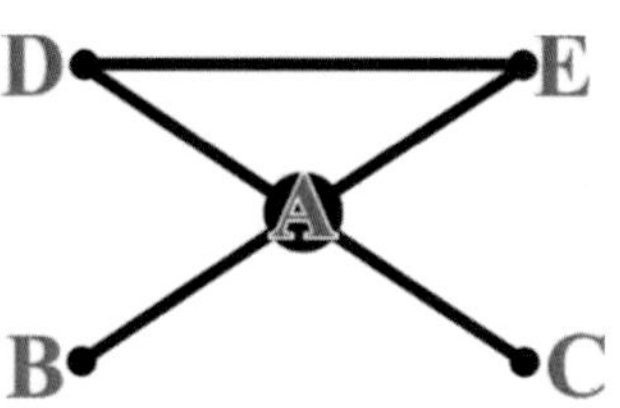

41, Continued

42: Step toward **E** with your left foot, ending up in an **X-stance** (kyocha sogi) with your left foot behind your right. Execute a **side poke** toward your right side, ending with the staff tucked under the left arm. **Kihap**.

42, Continued

42, Continued

42, Continued

42, Continued

43: Draw left leg up into a **one legged stance** (han bal sogi). Execute a **high-low classical pose** with the bottom hand open.

44: Put left foot down along line **EA**, facing **A** in a **left foot forward front stance** (wen bal ahp sogi). Execute a **high section double horizontal block**.

45: Step forward with your right foot into a **right foot forward front stance** (orun bal ahp sogi) and execute a right **lower section block**, ending with your left hand tucked under your right arm, and your right arm fully extended.

45, Continued

46: Step forward toward **A**, executing a counterclockwise **overhead spin**.

46, Continued

46, Continued

46, Continued

47: Land in a **left foot forward front stance** (wen bal ahp sogi) and execute a left **lower section block**, ending with your right hand tucked under your left arm, and your left arm fully extended.

47, Continued

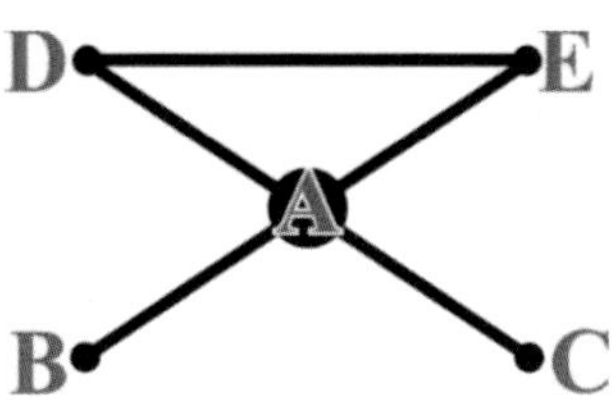

48: Bring your right foot up to your left foot in a transitional **closed stance** (moa sogi). Step out with your left foot and kneel down in a **left foot forward kneeling front stance** (wen bal murrup gurro sogi). Execute a **reverse high section poke**.

48, Continued

49: Maintain stance while executing a right to left **low section foot sweep**. (**Note**: this picture was taken from an alternate angle in order to improve the visibility of the technique.)

50: Execute a **downward strike**, with your left hand as the driver. **Kihap**.

51: ***Paro:*** Step up with your left foot into a **parallel stance** (narani sogi) at **A**, facing the front of the room. Execute a **slow pushing twin high section horizontal block**.

51, Continued

52: Maintain stance and execute a **twin low section horizontal block**.

**Ready Position:** Left Foot Moves to Closed Ready Stance Staff to Right Side.

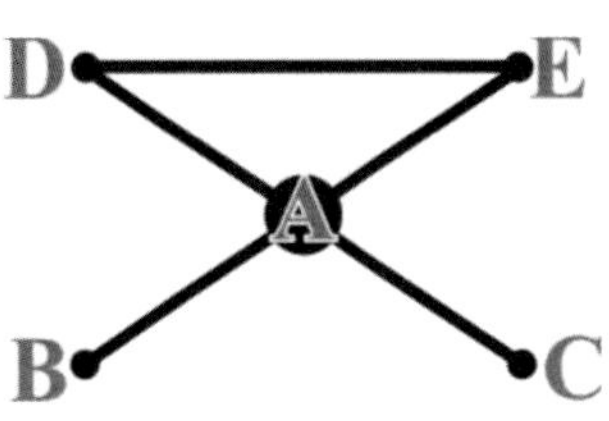

Bow, maintaining hand and weapon position

Students testing for red belt must know form Man Nam.

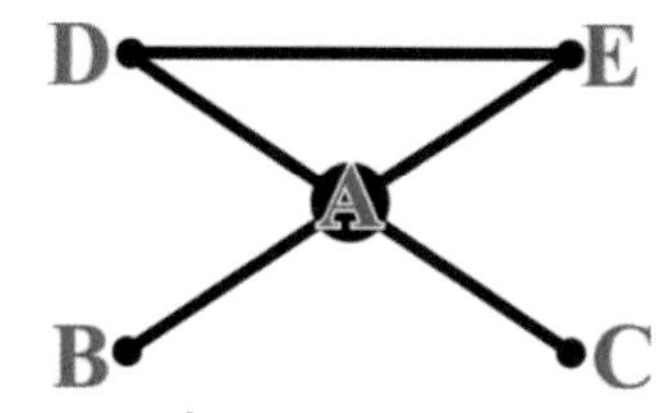


**Man Nam: Meet or Gather Together.** Learning from contact, we are the sum total of all the experiences we have had, represented by the coming together of the practitioner and the Bo staff.

**Ready Position:** Closed ready stance staff to right side at A facing forward.

**Movements:**

1: Step out with your left foot into a **parallel stance** (narani sogi) at **A**, facing the front of the room. Execute a **slow pushing twin high section horizontal block**. There is no **Kihap** on this move.

2: Maintain stance and execute a **twin low section horizontal block**.

3: Turn left toward **B** forming a **left foot forward front stance** (wen bal ahp sogi). As you are doing this, reverse your grip with your right hand and execute a **high section downward strike**. **Kihap**.

4: Shift your weight back and reset your grip with your right hand, forming a **left back stance** (wen bal dwi sogi) on line **AB** facing **B**. Execute a **classical box block**.

5: Bring your right foot forward into a transitional closed stance and let the staff drop to your right side. Step toward **B** with your left foot, forming a **left foot forward front stance** (wen bal ahp sogi). Execute a **reverse middle section poke**.

6: Note: the next three movements are done rapidly and illustrate **Body Conditioning**. Maintain stance. Execute a **low section strike**.

7: Maintain stance. Execute a **mid section strike**.

8: Maintain stance. Execute a **high section strike**.

9: Pivot on left foot and step right foot clockwise toward **A** and land in a **right foot forward front stance** (orun bal ahp sogi) along line **AB** facing **A**. Execute a **reverse middle section poke**.

10: Note: the next eight movements illustrate **Theory** and **Body Conditioning**. Step forward toward **E** into a **left foot forward front stance** (wen bal ahp sogi). Execute a **reverse middle section poke**.

11: Maintain stance and execute a **downward strike** toward the clavicle.

12: Maintain stance and execute a **reverse middle section poke**.

13: Maintain stance and execute an **upward strike** towards the groin.

14: Maintain stance and execute a **reverse middle section poke**.

15: Maintain stance and execute a **high section strike** (right to left), allowing the end of the staff to strike the outside of your arm.

16: Maintain stance and execute a **high section strike** (left to right), allowing the end of the staff to strike the outside of your arm.

17: Maintain stance and execute a **high section strike** (right to left), allowing the end of the staff to strike the outside of your arm.

18: Pivot on left foot and step right foot clockwise toward **C**, forming a **right foot forward front stance** (orun bal ahp sogi). As you are doing this, reverse your grip with your left hand and execute a **downward strike**. **Kihap**.

19: Shift your weight back and reset your grip with your left hand, forming a **right foot forward back stance** (orun bal dwi sogi) on line **AC** facing **C**. Execute a **classical box block**.

20: Bring your left foot forward into a transitional closed stance and let the staff drop to your left side. Step toward **C** with your right foot, forming a **right foot forward front stance** (orun bal ahp sogi). Execute a **reverse middle section poke**.

21: Note: the next three movements are done rapidly and illustrate **Body Conditioning**. Maintain stance. Execute a **low section strike**.

22: Maintain stance. Execute a **mid section strike**.

23: Maintain stance. Execute a **high section strike**.

24: Pivot on right foot and step left foot counterclockwise toward **A** and land in a **left foot forward front stance** (wen bal ahp sogi) along line **AC** facing **A**. Execute a **reverse middle section poke**.

25: Reverse grip with right hand and step forward toward **D**, forming a **right foot forward transitional stance**. Start executing a right hand **figure eight**. This is the first twirl.

26: Maintain stance. Continue executing right hand **figure eight**. This is the second twirl.

27: Maintain stance. Continue executing right hand **figure eight**. This is the third twirl.

28: Step forward toward **D**, forming a **left foot forward transitional stance**. Switch grip to left hand and begin executing a left hand **figure eight**. This is the first twirl.

29: Maintain stance. Continue executing left hand **figure eight**. This is the second twirl.

30: Maintain stance. Continue executing left hand **figure eight**. This is the third twirl.

31: Step forward into a **right foot forward front stance** (orun bal ahp sogi) while catching the staff on your right side. Execute a right **middle section poke**.

32: Step forward toward **D** into a **left foot forward front stance** (wen bal ahp sogi). Let go with your left hand and shift your left grip to the bottom of the staff. Execute an **overhead strike** down and to the left at a 45-degree angle. **Kihap**.

33: Draw right leg up into a **one legged stance** (han bal sogi). Execute a **high-low classical pose** with the bottom hand open.

34: Note: the next three moves are done together and illustrate **Manipulation**. Put your right foot down so that you are on line **DE** facing the front of the room. Slide your right hand to the center of the staff, palm inward. Turn your right hand clockwise, so that the palm faces away from you, causing the staff to spin 180-degrees.

35: Step clockwise with your left foot landing in a transitional **horse stance** (kima sogi) along line **DE** facing the back of the room. As you step, bring the staff behind your back and switch from a right grip to a left grip.

36: Bring the staff back in front of you with your left hand facing palm out. Put the back of your right hand against the staff, with your palm facing toward you. Use your left hand to spin the staff clockwise into your right hand. As you are doing this, step clockwise with your right foot ending up in a **right foot forward back stance** (orun bal dwi sogi) along line **DE**, facing **E**. While you are stepping, continue spinning the staff clockwise with your right hand. At the end of the spin allow the end of the staff to strike you in the back while you execute a left hand **reverse high section knifehand block** (sahngdan bahndae sohn-kal makgi).

37: Step forward with your left foot into a **left foot forward front stance** (wen bal ahp sogi). Pass the staff over your right shoulder, from your right hand to your left hand.

38: Maintain stance. Execute a **reverse middle section poke**.

39: Maintain stance. Execute a **low section foot sweep**, using your right hand to drive the staff.

40: Maintain stance. Execute a **reverse high section strike**, ending with the staff tucked under your right arm.

41: Bring your right foot to your left foot and execute a left leg **connecting front snap kick** (eeh oh ahp chagi). As you land, step toward **E** with your right foot, forming a transitional stance along line **DE**.

42: Step toward **E** with your left foot, ending up in an **X-stance** (kyocha sogi) with your left foot behind your right. Execute a **side poke** toward your right side, ending with the staff tucked under the left arm. **Kihap**.

43: Draw left leg up into a **one legged stance** (han bal sogi). Execute a **high-low classical pose** with the bottom hand open.

44: Put left foot down along line **EA**, facing **A** in a **left foot forward front stance** (wen bal ahp sogi). Execute a **high section double horizontal block**.

45: Step forward with your right foot into a **right foot forward front stance** (orun bal ahp sogi) and execute a right **lower section block**, ending with your left hand tucked under your right arm, and your right arm fully extended.

46: Step forward toward **A**, executing a counterclockwise **overhead spin**.

47: Land in a **left foot forward front stance** (wen bal ahp sogi) and execute a left **lower section block**, ending with your right hand tucked under your left arm, and your left arm fully extended.

48: Bring your right foot up to your left foot in a transitional **closed stance** (moa sogi). Step out with your left foot and kneel down in a **left foot forward kneeling front stance** (wen bal murrup gurro sogi). Execute a **reverse high section poke**.

49: Maintain stance while executing a right to left **low section foot sweep**. (**Note**: this picture was taken from an alternate angle in order to improve the visibility of the technique.)

50: Execute a **downward strike**, with your left hand as the driver. **Kihap**.

51: ***Paro:*** Step up with your left foot into a **parallel stance** (narani sogi) at **A**, facing the front of the room. Execute a **slow pushing twin high section horizontal block**.

52: Maintain stance and execute a **twin low section horizontal block**.

Return Left Leg to Ready Position.

# 가치

# Ka Chi

(36 Movements)
Presented by Master Rick Bjorkquist

**Ka Chi:** **Go Together.** Sharing the journey of life.

---

**Ready Position:** Parallel Stance. Execute a Middle Section Twin Vertical Spearhand Push.

1: Reach up with both hands and execute a sleeve and lapel grab. Pull downward and to your right, executing a **propping ankle throw** (sasae tsurikomi ashi) with your right foot. **Kihap**. Set your right foot down to form a transitional stance toward **B**.

C A B

1, Continued

2: Pivot on right foot toward **B** and execute a left **low section roundhouse kick** (hadan tollyo chagi).

3: Land in a **left foot forward front stance** (wen bal ahp sogi) facing **B**. Execute a right **reverse high section ridgehand strike** (sahngdan bahndae yuk sohn-kal darigi).

4: Move toward **B** with a right **rear leg hook kick** (dwi bal golcha chagi), landing in a transitional stance.

4, Continued

C A B

5: Execute a left **low section rear leg side thrust kick** (hadan dwi bal yup chagi). Land in a **left foot forward front stance** (wen bal ahp sogi) facing **B**.

6: Execute a sleeve and lapel grab followed by a **knee strike** with the right knee (murrup chagi).

7: Maintain stance and grip. Execute a second **knee strike** with the right knee (murrup chagi).

8: Step right foot behind left (facing **A**) and extend left leg while executing a **body drop throw** (tai otoshi) over the left leg.

8, Continued

8, Alternate View

8, Continued, Alternate View

C A B

9: Follow through with the throw by placing left knee on the ground and executing a right leg **foot sweep/drop spinning hook kick** (murrup gurro dwi tollyo golcha chagi) across line **AB** to your rear.

10: Keeping your weight on your left knee, pivot back so you are facing **A**. Execute a right leg **low section kneeling roundhouse kick** (hadan murrup gurro tollyo chagi) to the front/right of the room.

11: Set your right leg down, forming a **right leg forward kneeling front stance** (orun bal murrup gurro sogi) facing **A**. Execute a right hand **palm heel face block** (sohn-bahdahk olgool makgi) with your right hand pushing to the left.

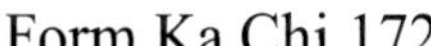

12: As you stand up into a **right foot forward front stance** (orun bal ahp sogi) execute a left hand **reverse middle section knifehand block** (chungdan bahndae sohn-kal makgi).

12, Continued

C — A — B

13: As you finish standing, execute a right hand **high section palm heel strike** (sahngdan sohn-bahdahk chirugi).

14: Maintain stance. Execute a right hand **middle section knifehand block** (chungdan sohn-kal makgi).

14, Continued

15: Maintain stance. Execute a left hand **reverse high section palm heel strike** (sahngdan bahndae sohn-bahdahk chirugi).

16: Maintain stance. Execute a right **high section front elbow strike** (sahngdan ahp palkumchi darigi). Do not strike left hand with right elbow.

17: Reach up with both hands and execute a sleeve and lapel grab. Pull downward and to your left, executing a **sliding ankle throw** (okuri ashi harai) with your left foot. **Kihap**. Set your left foot down to form a transitional stance toward **C**.

C —— A —— B

18: Pivot on left foot toward **C** and execute a right **low section roundhouse kick** (hadan tollyo chagi).

19: Land in a **right foot forward front stance** (orun bal ahp sogi) facing **C**. Execute a left **reverse high section ridgehand strike** (sahngdan bahndae yuk sohn-kal darigi).

20: Move toward **C** with a left **rear leg hook kick** (dwi bal golcha chagi), landing in a transitional stance.

20, Continued

21: Execute a right **low section rear leg side thrust kick** (hadan dwi bal yup chagi). Land in a **right foot forward front stance** (orun bal ahp sogi) facing **C**.

21, Continued

22: Execute a high section sleeve and label grab followed by a **knee strike** with the left knee (murrup chagi).

22, Continued

23: Maintain stance and grip. Execute a second **knee strike** with the left knee (murrup chagi).

C A B

23, Continued

24: Step left foot behind right (facing **A**) and extend right leg while executing a **body drop throw** (tai otoshi) over the right leg.

24, Continued

24, Alternate View

25: Follow through with the throw by placing right knee on the ground and executing a left leg **drop spinning hook kick** (murrup gurro dwi tollyo golcha chagi) across line **AC** to your rear.

25, Continued

C —— A —— B

25, Continued

26: Keeping your weight on your right knee, pivot back so you are facing **A**. Execute a left leg **kneeling roundhouse kick** (murrup gurro tollyo chagi) to the front/right of the room.

26, Continued

27: Set your left leg down, forming a **left leg forward kneeling front stance** (wen bal murrup gurro sogi) facing **A**. Execute a left hand **palm heel face block** (sohn-bahdahk olgool makgi) with your left hand pushing to the right.

28: As you stand up into a **left foot forward front stance** (wen bal ahp sogi) execute a right hand **reverse middle section knifehand block** (chungdan bahndae sohn-kal makgi).

28, Continued

29: As you finish standing, execute a left hand **high section palm heel strike** (sahngdan sohn-bahdahk chirugi).

30: Maintain stance. Execute a left hand **middle section knifehand block** (chungdan sohn-kal makgi).

C A B

30, Continued

31: Maintain stance. Execute a right hand **reverse high section palm heel strike** (sahngdan bahndae sohn-bahdahk chirugi).

32: Maintain stance. Execute a left **high section front elbow strike** (sahngdan ahp palkumchi darigi). Strike your right hand with your left elbow.

33: Step forward with your right foot, forming a **horse stance** (kima sogi) along line **AC** facing the front of the room. Execute an **X-grab trap** (kyocha olgami) by bringing your left hand out in a hooking block and your right hand across in a grab. Your end position should look similar to a knifehand X-block.

33, Continued

33, Continued

34: Maintain stance. Execute an **arm pull** (dan gigi) by pulling both hands downward to your right hip in a stacked position with the left hand open. This is an **arm wrench** (cho-igi).

34, Continued

34, Continued

34, Continued

C — A — B

34, Continued

35: Maintain stance. Execute a left **high section knifehand block** (sahngdan sohn-kal makgi). Simultaneously execute a right **high section uppercut** (sahngdan twijibo chirugi) to your opponent's chin.

35, Continued

35, Continued

36: Pull both hands back to your sides and execute a **high section twin thumb strike** (sahngdan sahng umji sohn garak chirugi). **Kihap**.

36, Continued

***Paro:*** Return Left Leg Ready Position. Execute a Middle Section Twin Vertical Spearhand Push.

Students testing for black stripe must know form Ka Chi.

**Ka Chi: Go Together.** Sharing the journey of life.
**Ready Position:** Parallel stance with middle section twin vertical spearhand push at A facing forward.
**Movements:**

1: Reach up with both hands and execute a sleeve and lapel grab. Pull downward and to your right, executing a **propping ankle throw** (sasae tsurikomi ashi) with your right foot. **Kihap**. Set your right foot down to form a transitional stance toward **B**.

2: Pivot on right foot toward **B** and execute a left **low section roundhouse kick** (hadan tollyo chagi).

3: Land in a **left foot forward front stance** (wen bal ahp sogi) facing **B**. Execute a right **reverse high section ridgehand strike** (sahngdan bahndae yuk sohn-kal darigi).

4: Move toward **B** with a right **rear leg hook kick** (dwi bal golcha chagi), landing in a transitional stance.

5: Execute a left **low section rear leg side thrust kick** (hadan dwi bal yup chagi). Land in a **left foot forward front stance** (wen bal ahp sogi) facing **B**.

6: Execute a sleeve and lapel grab followed by a **knee strike** with the right knee (murrup chagi).

7: Maintain stance and grip. Execute a second **knee strike** with the right knee (murrup chagi).

8: Step right foot behind left (facing **A**) and extend left leg while executing a **body drop throw** (tai otoshi) over the left leg.

9: Follow through with the throw by placing left knee on the ground and executing a right leg **foot sweep/drop spinning hook kick** (murrup gurro dwi tollyo golcha chagi) across line **AB** to your rear.

10: Keeping your weight on your left knee, pivot back so you are facing **A**. Execute a right leg **low section kneeling roundhouse kick** (hadan murrup gurro tollyo chagi) to the front/right of the room.

11: Set your right leg down, forming a **right leg forward kneeling front stance** (orun bal murrup gurro sogi) facing **A**. Execute a right hand **palm heel face block** (sohn-bahdahk olgool makgi) with your right hand pushing to the left.

12: As you stand up into a **right foot forward front stance** (orun bal ahp sogi) execute a left hand **reverse middle section knifehand block** (chungdan bahndae sohn-kal makgi).

13: As you finish standing, execute a right hand **high section palm heel strike** (sahngdan sohn-bahdahk chirugi).

14: Maintain stance. Execute a right hand **middle section knifehand block** (chungdan sohn-kal makgi).

15: Maintain stance. Execute a left hand **reverse high section palm heel strike** (sahngdan bahndae sohn-bahdahk chirugi).

16: Maintain stance. Execute a right **high section front elbow strike** (sahngdan ahp palkumchi darigi). Do not strike left hand with right elbow.

17: Reach up with both hands and execute a sleeve and lapel grab. Pull downward and to your left, executing a **sliding ankle throw** (okuri ashi harai) with your left foot. **Kihap**. Set your left foot down to form a transitional stance toward **C**.

18: Pivot on left foot toward **C** and execute a right **low section roundhouse kick** (hadan tollyo chagi).

19: Land in a **right foot forward front stance** (orun bal ahp sogi) facing **C**. Execute a left **reverse high section ridgehand strike** (sahngdan bahndae yuk sohn-kal darigi).

20: Move toward **C** with a left **rear leg hook kick** (dwi bal golcha chagi), landing in a transitional stance.

21: Execute a right **low section rear leg side thrust kick** (hadan dwi bal yup chagi). Land in a **right foot forward front stance** (orun bal ahp sogi) facing **C**.

22: Execute a high section sleeve and label grab followed by a **knee strike** with the left knee (murrup chagi).

23: Maintain stance and grip. Execute a second **knee strike** with the left knee (murrup chagi).

24: Step left foot behind right (facing **A**) and extend right leg while executing a **body drop throw** (tai otoshi) over the right leg.

25: Follow through with the throw by placing right knee on the ground and executing a left leg **drop spinning hook kick** (murrup gurro dwi tollyo golcha chagi) across line **AC** to your rear.

26: Keeping your weight on your right knee, pivot back so you are facing **A**. Execute a left leg **kneeling roundhouse kick** (murrup gurro tollyo chagi) to the front/right of the room.

27: Set your left leg down, forming a **left leg forward kneeling front stance** (wen bal murrup gurro sogi) facing **A**. Execute a left hand **palm heel face block** (sohn-bahdahk olgool makgi) with your left hand pushing to the right.

28: As you stand up into a **left foot forward front stance** (wen bal ahp sogi) execute a right hand **reverse middle section knifehand block** (chungdan bahndae sohn-kal makgi).

29: As you finish standing, execute a left hand **high section palm heel strike** (sahngdan sohn-bahdahk chirugi).

30: Maintain stance. Execute a left hand **middle section knifehand block** (chungdan sohn-kal makgi).

31: Maintain stance. Execute a right hand **reverse high section palm heel strike** (sahngdan bahndae sohn-bahdahk chirugi).

32: Maintain stance. Execute a left **high section front elbow strike** (sahngdan ahp palkumchi darigi). Strike your right hand with your left elbow.

33: Step forward with your right foot, forming a **horse stance** (kima sogi) along line **AC** facing the front of the room. Execute an **X-grab trap** (kyocha olgami) by bringing your left hand out in a hooking block and your right hand across in a grab. Your end position should look similar to a knifehand X-block.

34: Maintain stance. Execute an **arm pull** (dan gigi) by pulling both hands downward to your right hip in a stacked position with the left hand open. This is an **arm wrench** (cho-igi).

35: Maintain stance. Execute a left **high section knifehand block** (sahngdan sohn-kal makgi). Simultaneously execute a right **high section uppercut** (sahngdan twijibo chirugi) to your opponent's chin.

36: Pull both hands back to your sides and execute a **high section twin thumb strike** (sahngdan sahng umji sohn garak chirugi). **Kihap**.

***Paro:*** Return Left Leg to Ready Position.

# 사랑

# Sa Rang

(33 Movements)
Presented by Master Jeffrey Kim

**Sa Rang:** **Love.** The willingness to sacrifice yourself for the benefit of someone or something in which you believe.

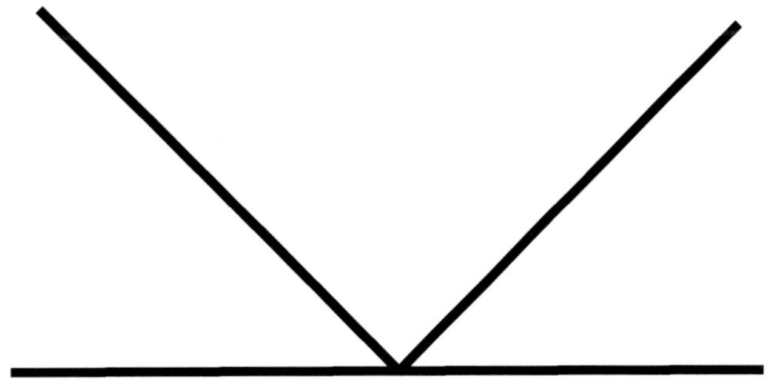

**Ready Position:** Parallel Stance Hands Open Crossed Over Chest Left Over Right

1: Left foot moves toward **B** to form a **left foot forward back stance** (wen bal dwi sogi). Execute a left **inside forearm block** (chungdan ahn palmok makgi). **Kihap**.

2: Maintain stance. Execute a right **reverse middle section turning punch** (chungdan bahndae tollyo ahp joomok chirugi).

3: Step forward toward **B**, forming a **right foot forward front stance** (orun bal ahp sogi). Execute a right slow (tahn jeon) **middle section knifehand block** (chungdan sohn-kal makgi) without a chambering X.

3, Continued

4: Maintain stance. Execute a left **reverse middle section front punch** (chungdan bahndae ahp joomok chirugi).

5: Execute a **low section rear leg side thrust kick** (hadan dwi bal yup chagi) toward **B**. Set left foot down into a transitional stance.

5, Continued

6: Turn clockwise and execute a **tornado kick** (toneido chagi) toward **B**. Right leg is the driver and left leg kicks.

6, Continued

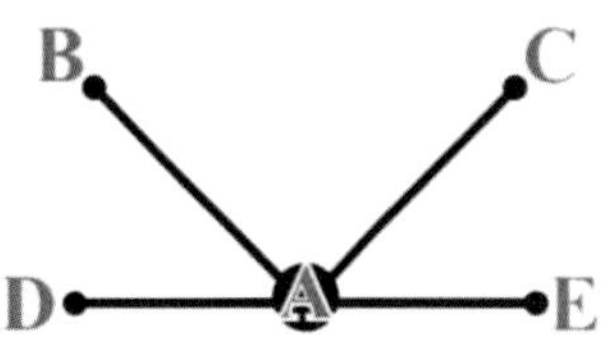

6, Continued

6, Continued

7: Land in a **left foot forward back stance** (wen bal dwi sogi) facing **B**. Execute a left hand **high section downward backfist strike** (sahngdan naeryo deung joomok darigi) toward **B**. This technique should strike downwards rather than across.

7, Continued

8: Pivot on your left foot and step with your right foot into a **horse stance** (kima sogi) along line **AB** and execute a right **high section outward knifehand strike** (sahngdan bakuro sohn-kal darigi) toward **A**. Note chambering position.

8, Continued

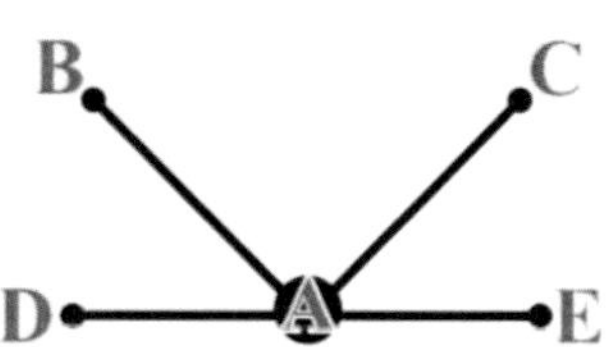


9: Turn your right hand so the thumb is up. Execute a left **outside to inside crescent kick** (ahp tollyo chagi), striking your right palm with the inside edge of your foot. Set down in a **horse stance** (kima sogi) along line **AB**, with your left foot closest to **A**.

9, Continued

10: Maintain stance and execute a left **high section front elbow strike** (sahngdan ahp palkumchi darigi), striking your right palm with your elbow.

10, Alternate View

11: Maintain stance and execute a left **middle section knifehand block** (chungdan sohn-kal makgi).

12: Step right leg 180 degrees counterclockwise toward **A**, forming a **horse stance** (kima sogi) along line **AB**. Execute a right **middle section side punch** (chungdan yup joomok chirugi).

13: Return left foot to **chunbi position**, but this time the right hand is over the left.

14: Right foot moves toward **C** to form a **right foot forward back stance** (orun bal dwi sogi). Execute a right **inside forearm block** (chungdan ahn palmok makgi). **Kihap**.

15: Maintain stance. Execute a left **reverse middle section turning punch** (chungdan bahndae tollyo ahp joomok chirugi).

16: Step forward toward **C**, forming a **left foot forward front stance** (wen bal ahp sogi). Execute a left slow (tahn jeon) **middle section knifehand block** (chungdan sohn-kal makgi) without a chambering X.

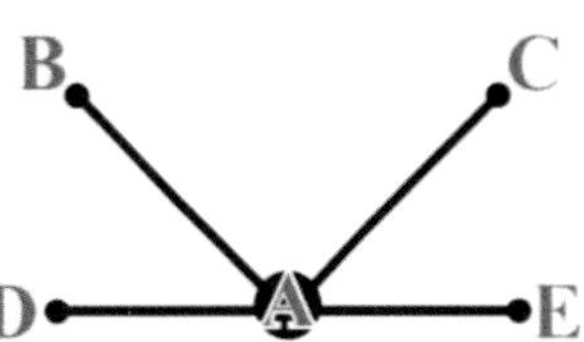

16, Continued

17: Maintain stance. Execute a right **reverse middle section front punch** (chungdan bahndae ahp joomok chirugi).

18: Execute a **low section rear leg side thrust kick** (hadan dwi bal yup chagi) toward **C**. Set right foot down into a transitional stance.

18, Continued

19: Turn clockwise and execute a **tornado kick** (toneido chagi) toward **C**. Left leg is the driver and right leg kicks.

19, Continued

19, Continued

19, Continued

20: Land in a **right foot forward back stance** (orun bal dwi sogi) facing **C**. Execute a right hand **high section downward backfist strike** (sahngdan naeryo deung joomok darigi) toward **C**. This technique should strike downwards rather than across.

20, Continued

21: Pivot on your right foot and step with your left foot into a **horse stance** (kima sogi) along line **AC** and execute a left **high section outward knifehand strike** (sahngdan bakuro sohn-kal darigi) toward **A**. Note chambering position.

21, Continued

22: Turn your left hand so the thumb is up. Execute a right **outside to inside crescent kick** (ahp tollyo chagi), striking your left palm with the inside edge of your foot. Set down in a **horse stance** (kima sogi) along line **AC**, with your right foot closest to **A**.

22, Continued

23: Maintain stance and execute a right **high section front elbow strike** (sahngdan ahp palkumchi darigi), striking your left palm with your elbow.

23, Alternate View

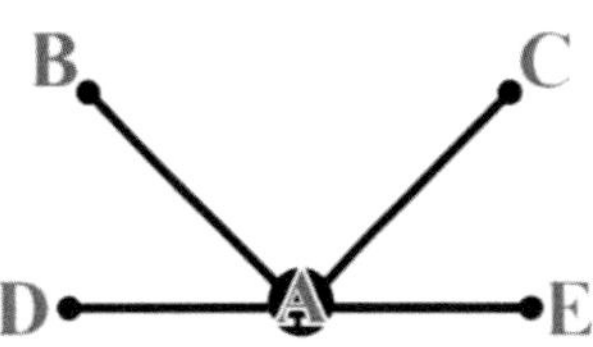

24: Maintain stance and execute a right **middle section knifehand block** (chungdan sohn-kal makgi).

25: Step left leg 180 degrees clockwise toward **A**, forming a **horse stance** (kima sogi) along line **AC**. Execute a left **middle section side punch** (chungdan yup joomok chirugi).

26: Shift right foot toward left foot and left foot toward **D**, forming a deep **left leg forward front stance** (wen bal ahp sogi). Stack your hands at your right hip and execute a **middle section twin palm heel pushing block (a "push the rock" block)** (chungdan sahng sohn-bahdahk miro makgi).

26, Continued

26, Continued

27: Execute a right leg **front snap kick** (ahp chagi) toward **D**.

27, Continued

28: Land in a **right foot forward front stance** (orun bal ahp sogi), executing a **high section inward twin knifehand strike** (sahngdan anuro sahng sohn-kal darigi).

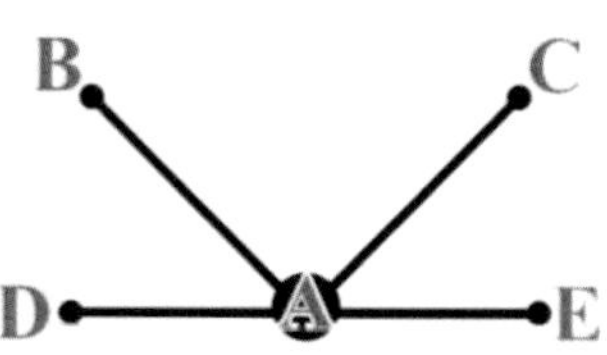

28, Continued

29: Move right foot over to the left and pivot on right foot 180-degrees counterclockwise toward **E**, forming a **left foot forward front stance** (wen bal ahp sogi) facing **A** Execute a right **reverse high section four knuckle strike** (sahngdan bahndae pyung joomok chirugi), with your left hand ending up under your right elbow.

29, Continued (Note clearing press with left hand)

29, Continued

29, Continued

30: Step right foot to meet left, and then step forward with right foot toward **E**, forming a deep **right leg forward front stance** (orun bal ahp sogi). Stack your hands at your left hip and execute a **middle section twin palm heel pushing block (a "push the rock" block)** (chungdan sahng sohn-bahdahk miro makgi).

30, Continued

30, Continued

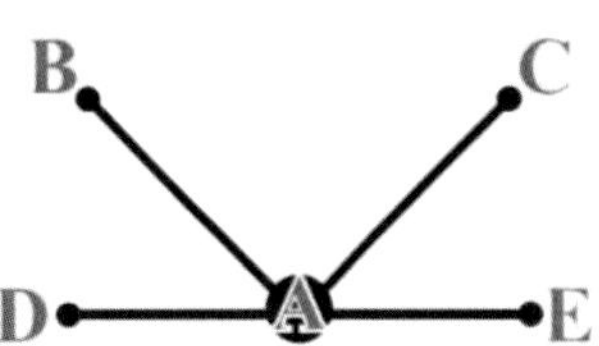

31: Execute a left leg **front snap kick** (ahp chagi) toward **E**.

31, Continued

32: Land in a **left foot forward front stance** (wen bal ahp sogi), executing a **high section inward twin knifehand strike** (sahngdan anuro sahng sohn-kal darigi).

32, Continued

33: Move left foot over to the right and pivot on left foot 180-degrees toward **D**, forming a **right foot forward front stance** (orun bal ahp sogi) facing **D**. Execute a left **reverse high section four knuckle strike** (sahngdan bahndae pyung joomok chirugi), with your right hand ending up under your left elbow. **Kihap**.

33, Continued (Note clearing press with left hand)

33, Continued

33, Continued

***Paro:*** Return Left Leg to Ready Position.Parallel Stance Hands Open Crossed Over Chest Left over Right

Students testing for black belt must know form Sa Rang.

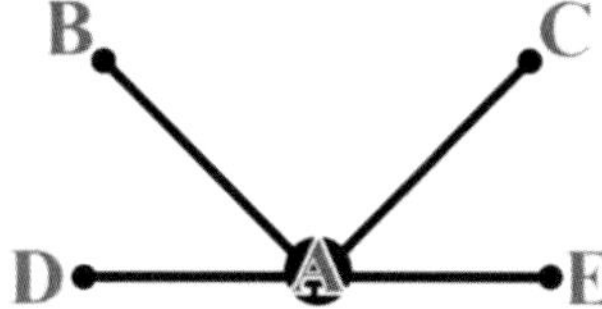


**Sa Rang: Love.** The willingness to sacrifice yourself for the benefit of someone or something in which you believe.

**Ready Position:** Parallel stance hands open crossed over chest left over right at A facing D.

**Movements:**

1: Left foot moves toward **B** to form a **left foot forward back stance** (wen bal dwi sogi). Execute a left **inside forearm block** (chungdan ahn palmok makgi). **Kihap**.

2: Maintain stance. Execute a right **reverse middle section turning punch** (chungdan bahndae tollyo ahp joomok chirugi).

3: Step forward toward **B**, forming a **right foot forward front stance** (orun bal ahp sogi). Execute a right slow (tahn jeon) **middle section knifehand block** (chungdan sohn-kal makgi).

4: Maintain stance. Execute a left **reverse middle section front punch** (chungdan bahndae ahp joomok chirugi).

5: Execute a **low section rear leg side thrust kick** (hadan dwi bal yup chagi) toward **B**. Set left foot down into a transitional stance.

6: Turn clockwise and execute a **tornado kick** (toneido chagi) toward **B**. Right leg is the driver and left leg kicks.

7: Land in a **left foot forward back stance** (wen bal dwi sogi) facing **B**. Execute a left hand **high section downward backfist strike** (sahngdan naeryo deung joomok darigi) toward **B**. This technique should strike downwards rather than across.

8: Pivot on your left foot and step with your right foot into a **horse stance** (kima sogi) along line **AB** and execute a right **high section outward knifehand strike** (sahngdan bakuro sohn-kal darigi) toward **A**.

9: Turn your right hand so the thumb is up. Execute a left **outside to inside crescent kick** (ahp tollyo chagi), striking your right palm with the inside edge of your foot. Set down in a **horse stance** (kima sogi) along line **AB**, with your left foot closest to **A**.

10: Maintain stance and execute a left **high section front elbow strike** (sahngdan ahp palkumchi darigi), striking your right palm with your elbow.

11: Maintain stance and execute a left **middle section knifehand block** (chungdan sohn-kal makgi).

12: Step right leg 180 degrees counterclockwise toward **A**, forming a **horse stance** (kima sogi) along line **AB**. Execute a right **middle section side punch** (chungdan yup joomok chirugi).

13: Return left foot to **chunbi position**, but this time the right hand is over the left.

14: Right foot moves toward **C** to form a **right foot forward back stance** (orun bal dwi sogi). Execute a right **inside forearm block** (chungdan ahn palmok makgi). **Kihap**.

15: Maintain stance. Execute a left **reverse middle section turning punch** (chungdan bahndae tollyo ahp joomok chirugi).

16: Step forward toward **C**, forming a **left foot forward front stance** (wen bal ahp sogi). Execute a left slow (tahn jeon) **middle section knifehand block** (chungdan sohn-kal makgi).

17: Maintain stance. Execute a right **reverse middle section front punch** (chungdan bahndae ahp joomok chirugi).

18: Execute a **low section rear leg side thrust kick** (hadan dwi bal yup chagi) toward **C**. Set right foot down into a transitional stance.

19: Turn clockwise and execute a **tornado kick** (toneido chagi) toward **C**. Left leg is the driver and right leg kicks.

20: Land in a **right foot forward back stance** (orun bal dwi sogi) facing **C**. Execute a right hand **high section downward backfist strike** (sahngdan naeryo deung joomok darigi) toward **C**. This technique should strike downwards rather than across.

21: Pivot on your right foot and step with your left foot into a **horse stance** (kima sogi) along line **AC** and execute a left **high section outward knifehand strike** (sahngdan bakuro sohn-kal darigi) toward **A**.

22: Turn your left hand so the thumb is up. Execute a right **outside to inside crescent kick** (ahp tollyo chagi), striking your left palm with the inside edge of your foot. Set down in a **horse stance** (kima sogi) along line **AC**, with your right foot closest to **A**.

23: Maintain stance and execute a right **high section front elbow strike** (sahngdan ahp palkumchi darigi), striking your left palm with your elbow.

24: Maintain stance and execute a right **middle section knifehand block** (chungdan sohn-kal makgi).

25: Step left leg 180 degrees clockwise toward **A**, forming a **horse stance** (kima sogi) along line **AC**. Execute a left **middle section side punch** (chungdan yup joomok chirugi).

26: Shift right foot toward left foot and left foot toward **D**, forming a deep **left leg forward front stance** (wen bal ahp sogi). Stack your hands at your right hip and execute a **middle section twin palm heel pushing block (a "push the rock" block)** (chungdan sahng sohn-bahdahk miro makgi).

27: Execute a right leg **front snap kick** (ahp chagi) toward **D**.

28: Land in a **right foot forward front stance** (orun bal ahp sogi), executing a **high section inward twin knifehand strike** (sahngdan anuro sahng sohn-kal darigi).

29: Move right foot over to the left and pivot on right foot 180-degrees counterclockwise toward **A**, forming a **left foot forward front stance** (wen bal ahp sogi) facing **E**. Execute a right **reverse high section four knuckle strike** (sahngdan bahndae pyung joomok chirugi), with your left hand ending up under your right elbow.

30: Step right foot to meet left, and then step forward with right foot toward **E**, forming a deep **right leg forward front stance** (orun bal ahp sogi). Stack your hands at your left hip and execute a **middle section twin palm heel pushing block (a "push the rock" block)** (chungdan sahng sohn-bahdahk miro makgi).

31: Execute a left leg **front snap kick** (ahp chagi) toward **E**.

32: Land in a **left foot forward front stance** (wen bal ahp sogi), executing a **high section inward twin knifehand strike** (sahngdan anuro sahng sohn-kal darigi).

33: Move left foot over to the right and pivot on left foot 180-degrees toward **D**, forming a **right foot forward front stance** (orun bal ahp sogi) facing **D**. Execute a left **reverse high section four knuckle strike** (sahngdan bahndae pyung joomok chirugi), with your right hand ending up under your left elbow. **Kihap**.

***Paro:*** Return Left Leg to Ready Position.

# 격기도낙법형

# Kyuki-Do Nakbop

(12 Movements)
Presented by Master Joe Moniot

**Kyuki-Do Nakbop Hyung:** Kyuki-Do Form of Falling

**Ready Position:** Parallel Stance.

1: Begin by executing a standing **back fall** (koho ukemi).

1, Continued

2: Without putting your legs down, proceed directly to a supine **left side fall** (hidari sokuho ukemi).

2, Continued

3: Toss your hips up into the air and execute a supine **right side fall** (migi sokuho ukemi). Post on your right arm and swing your right leg back to a kneeling position with the left knee up. Drop the left knee next to the right.

3, Continued

3, Continued

3, Continued

3, Continued

3, Continued

4: Execute a kneeling **front fall** (zenpo ukemi). Tuck your right knee to your chest and step your left leg into a kneeling position with the left knee up. Stand up and step your left leg back into a **closed stance** (moa sogi). Extend your right arm straight out from your body.

4, Continued

4, Continued

4, Continued

4, Continued

5: Step forward with your left foot into a **left foot forward front stance** (wen bal ahp sogi). Swing your right leg and right arm toward your left foot and execute a **standing right side fall** (tachi migi sokuho ukemi). Post on your right arm and come to your feet by swinging your right leg back. Step back with the left leg into a **closed stance** (moa sogi). Extend your left arm straight out from your body.

5, Continued

5, Continued

5, Continued

5, Continued

5, Continued

5, Continued

5, Continued

5, Continued

6: Step forward with your right foot into a **right foot forward front stance** (orun bal ahp sogi). Swing your left leg and left arm toward your right foot and execute a **standing left side fall** (tachi hidari sokuho ukemi). Post on your left arm and come to your feet by swinging your left leg back. Step back with the right leg into a **parallel stance** (narani sogi).

6, Continued

6, Continued

6, Continued

6, Continued

6, Continued

6, Continued

6, Continued

7: Execute a **standing front fall** (tachi zenpo ukemi). Tuck your right knee to your chest and come up to a kneeling position with the left knee up. As you stand, shift into a **left foot forward back stance** (wen bal dwi sogi).

7, Continued

7, Continued

7, Continued

7, Continued

8: Reach toward **B** with your right arm and step forward into a **standing right forward rolling fall** (tachi migi zenpo kaiten). Land in the sidefall position. Post on your left arm and come to your feet by swinging your left leg back, standing up into a **right foot forward back stance** facing **B**. Step clockwise toward **B** with your left leg, turning 180-degrees into a **right foot forward back stance** (orun bal dwi sogi) facing **A**.

8, Continued

8, Continued

8, Continued

8, Continued

8, Continued

8, Continued

8, Continued

9: Reach toward **A** with your left arm and step forward into a **standing left forward rolling fall** (tachi hidari zenpo kaiten). Land in the sidefall position. Post on your right arm and come to your feet by swinging your right leg back, standing up into a **left foot forward back stance** facing **A**. Step counterclockwise toward **A** with your right leg, turning 180-degrees into a **left foot forward back stance** (wen bal dwi sogi) facing **B**.

9, Continued

9, Continued

9, Continued

9, Continued

9, Continued

9, Continued

9, Continued

9, Continued

9, Continued

10: Reach toward **B** with your right arm and step forward into a **standing right forward rolling fall** (tachi migi zenpo kaiten). Roll directly to your feet, shifting your feet clockwise to face **A** in a **right foot forward back stance** (orun bal dwi sogi).

10, Continued

10, Continued

10, Continued

10, Continued

10, Continued

11: Reach toward **A** with your left arm and step forward into a **standing left forward rolling fall** (tachi hidari zenpo kaiten). Roll directly to your feet, shifting your feet counterclockwise to face **B** in a **left foot forward back stance** (wen bal dwi sogi). Step back with the left foot into a **parallel stance** (narani sogi).

11, Continued

11, Continued

11, Continued

11, Continued

11, Continued

11, Continued

12: Execute a handstand or somersault into a **back fall** (koho ukemi). Land with the back very slightly arched. Pause briefly. Sit up.

12, Continued

12, Continued

12, Continued

12, Continued

***Paro:*** Execute a backward shoulder roll over the right shoulder and stand up in a **Parallel Stance** (chunbi) at **A** facing **B**.

Paro, Continued

Paro, Continued

Paro, Continued

Paro, Continued

Students testing for black belt must know form Kyuki-Do Nakbop.

**Kyuki-Do Nakbop:** Kyuki-Do Form of Falling.
**Ready Position:** Parallel stance at A facing B.
**Movements:**

1: Begin by executing a standing **back fall** (koho ukemi).

2: Without putting your legs down, proceed directly to a supine **left side fall** (hidari sokuho ukemi).

3: Toss your hips up into the air and execute a supine **right side fall** (migi sokuho ukemi). Post on your right arm and swing your right leg back to a kneeling position with the left knee up. Drop the left knee.

4: Execute a **kneeling front fall** (zenpo ukemi). Tuck your right knee to your chest and step your left leg into a kneeling position with the left knee up. Stand up and step your left leg back into a closed stance (moa sogi). Extend your right arm straight out from your body. 5: Step forward with your left foot into a **left foot forward front stance** (wen bal ahp sogi). Swing your right leg and right arm toward your left foot and execute a **standing right side fall** (tachi migi sokuho ukemi). Post on your right arm and come to your feet by swinging your right leg back. Step back with the left leg into a **closed stance** (moa sogi). Extend your left arm straight out from your body.

6: Step forward with your right foot into a **right foot forward front stance** (orun bal ahp sogi). Swing your left leg and left arm toward your right foot and execute a **standing left side fall** (tachi hidari sokuho ukemi). Post on your left arm and come to your feet by swinging your left leg back. Step back with the right leg into a **parallel stance** (narani sogi).

7: Execute a **standing front fall** (tachi zenpo ukemi). Tuck your right knee to your chest and come up to a kneeling position with the left knee up. As you stand, shift into a **left foot forward back stance** (wen bal dwi sogi).

8: Reach toward **B** with your right arm and step forward into a **standing right forward rolling fall** (tachi migi zenpo kaiten). Land in the sidefall position. Post on your left arm and come to your feet by swinging your left leg back, standing up into a **right foot forward back stance** facing **B**. Step clockwise toward **B** with your left leg, turning 180-degrees into a **right foot forward back stance** (orun bal dwi sogi) facing **A**.

9: Reach toward **A** with your left arm and step forward into a **standing left forward rolling fall** (tachi hidari zenpo kaiten). Land in the sidefall position. Post on your right arm and come to your feet by swinging your right leg back, standing up into a **left foot forward back stance** facing **A**. Step counterclockwise toward **A** with your right leg, turning 180-degrees into a **left foot forward back stance** (wen bal dwi sogi) facing **B**.

10: Reach toward **B** with your right arm and step forward into a **standing right forward rolling fall** (tachi migi zenpo kaiten). Roll directly to your feet, shifting your feet clockwise to face **A** in a right **foot forward back stance** (orun bal dwi sogi).

11: Reach toward **A** with your left arm and step forward into a **standing left forward rolling fall** (tachi hidari zenpo kaiten). Roll directly to your feet, shifting your feet counterclockwise to face **B** in a **left foot forward back stance** (wen bal dwi sogi). Step back with the left foot into a **parallel stance** (narani sogi).

12: Execute a handstand or somersault into a **back fall** (koho ukemi). Land with the back very slightly arched. Pause briefly. Sit up.

***Paro:*** Execute a backward shoulder roll over the right shoulder and stand up in a **Parallel Stance** (chunbi) at **A** facing **B**.

# Chapter Seven: Grand Master Ken Ok Hyung Kim

Grand Master Kim was born on May 20th, 1939 in Ansong, Korea, just south of the 38th parallel. He began training in the martial arts in 1949. Master Kim joined the Korean navy in 1959; he specialized in underwater demolitions and served until 1962. In 1959, Master Kim became the Civilian Instructor for the United States 8th Army in Korea, teaching Judo, Karate and self-defense.

In 1963 he graduated from the Korean Sports and Science College of Seoul (now called Yongin, the Yudo College). His degree was in physical education, and he went on to serve as an assistant instructor at the college.

In 1966 he was awarded his 5th Dan in Judo and in Tang Soo Do from the Korean Judo Association and Korean Tang Soo Do Association. In 1967 he came to the United States to teach martial arts, serving as the chief instructor at Elgin Judo and Karate (a subsidiary of the Military Arts Institute of Chicago).

In 1968 he attended George Williams College, focusing his studies on physical education. In this same year, he opened his own school (Kim's Black Belt Academy in Elgin, Illinois, teaching Tae Kwon Do and Judo) as well as teaching physical education at the Elgin Community College and serving on the Promotional Testing Committee of the U.S. Judo Federation.

In 1970 he was promoted to 6th Dan Master Black Belt in Tae Kwon Do by the Korean Tae Kwon Do Association. He was also a founding member of the American Tae Kwon Do Federation and served as their first Secretary General. During this year he also became Elgin Community College's wrestling coach, a position that he held for the next three years.

In 1974 he was promoted to $6^{th}$ Dan Master Black Belt in Judo by the Korean Judo Association, and in 1975 he was promoted to $7^{th}$ Dan in Tae Kwon Do by the American Tae Kwon Do Federation. In that same year he served as the first Vice President of the American Tae Kwon Do Federation.

In 1976 he was promoted to $8^{th}$ Dan by the American Tae Kwon Do Federation. This same year he left the American Tae Kwon Do Federation to begin the founding of the AKF (American Kyuki-Do Federation). It was three years later (in 1979) that the AKF was formally founded (this was the first year that the Federation held a Kyuki-Do tournament and began promoting students in Kyuki-Do as its own martial art).

In 1980, the AKF board of directors promoted him to $8^{th}$ Dan, Grand Master in Kyuki-Do, and in 1985 the International Council on Martial Arts Education promoted him to $9^{th}$ Dan in Tae Kwon Do.

From 1989 to 1991 Grand Master Kim served as the president of the Alumni Association of the Korean Sports and Science College. In 1990 he was promoted to $7^{th}$ Dan Head Master in Judo by the Korean Judo Association.

In 1992 the AKF board of directors promoted him to $9^{th}$ Dan Grand Master in Kyuki-Do. In this year he was also awarded the rank of $9^{th}$ degree Grand Master in Karate from Grand Master Soon Ho Chang of Philadelphia, Pennsylvania. In 2004 he was awarded the rank of $9^{th}$ Dan Grand Master in Judo by the AKF, and in 2010 he was promoted to $10^{th}$ Dan Grand Master in Kyuki-Do by the AKF.

Grand Master Kim has been active in martial arts tournaments since coming to the United States in 1967. He has officiated and promoted Tae Kwon Do, Judo and Kyuki-Do tournaments. In addition to traveling throughout the United States, Grand Master Kim has repeatedly traveled to Korea, Mexico, England, Scotland, Japan and Greece in his quest to promote and improve the martial arts. He places a tremendous emphasis on the importance of family, community and education, and this philosophy is reflected in every aspect of the art.

Grand Master Kim is currently retired, but he remains committed to continually promoting and improving the art of Kyuki-Do and to helping others grow, mature and better themselves and society through the understanding and practice of the martial arts.

# Chapter Eight: Appendices

# *Appendix A: Korean Terminology*

One of the unique aspects of the martial arts is its reach into a culture and custom far different from our own. This is reflected in the various terminologies the different styles use. The student, through the study of terminology, is given the opportunity to discover and catch a glimpse of different and fascinating cultures and customs. One not only realizes the uniqueness of the discipline, but also becomes unique as a result of it.

Terminology is a communication tool by which the student slowly learns to respect and comprehend the depth of Kyuki-Do. Through the study of terminology, the spirit of Kyuki-Do spreads and builds to unite its students as one, joining them to one discipline.

Use of proper terminology shows respect for the origins of Kyuki-Do and is encouraged at all times. At higher ranks, students will be expected to demonstrate a clear comprehension of the Korean terminology used to describe different techniques. A summary of this terminology follows.

## Terminology: Fighting Arts

| | |
|---|---|
| Kyuki-Do | **Kyuk-** spark or sudden explosion **Ki-** mental/physical/spiritual energy **Do-** art/way |
| Mudo | Korean term for the warrior's path or way (Budo in Japanese) |
| Tae Kwon Do | Korean martial art using the hands and feet in self-defense **Tae-** foot **Kwon-** fist **Do-** art/way/method |
| Judo (Yudo) | Means "gentle way," the art of grappling, throwing and ground fighting |
| Hapkido | Korean art of joint locks, pressure points, and pain compliance **Hap-** unite **Ki-** energy **Do-** art/way |
| Jiu Jitsu | Means gentle/yielding method/style |
| Ma Eum | Mind |
| Mohm | Body (may also be called Yukche) |
| Jung Shin | Spirit |

## Terminology: General

| <u>English</u> | <u>Korean</u> |
|---|---|
| Sparring | Daeryun (deh-rhee-uhn) |
| Free sparring (free fighting) | Chayu daeryon |
| Free style one-step sparring | Chayu ilbo daeryon |
| One-step sparring | Ilbo daeryon |
| Two-step sparring | Ebo daeryon |
| Three-step sparring | Sambo daeryon |
| Director | Kwanjang-nim |

| | |
|---|---|
| Instructor | Sahbum-nim |
| Student | Jeja |
| Degree | Dan |
| Degree holder | Yudanja |
| Grade | Kup |
| Grade holder | Yukupja |
| Uniform | Dobok |
| Uniform top | Sahng-wee |
| Uniform bottom | Ha-wee |
| Belt | Dee |
| Training hall | Dojang |
| Yell/shout | Kihap |
| Forms | Hyung |
| Flag | Kuki |
| Korean flag | Taeguk ki |
| Korean alphabet | Hangul |

## Terminology: Body Parts

| **English** | **Korean** |
|---|---|
| Foot | Bal (emphasize softly) |
| Leg | Da-ri |
| Arm | Pal (emphasize hard) |
| Neck | Mok |
| Forearm | Palmok |
| Fist | Joomok |
| Hand | Sohn |
| Knifehand | Sohn-kal |
| Ridgehand | Yuk sohn-kal |
| Fingers | Sohn-garak |
| Finger tip | Sohn-gut |
| Elbow | Palkumchi |
| Knee | Murrup |

## Terminology: Direction, Location and Movement

| **English** | **Korean** |
|---|---|
| Right | Orun |
| Left | Wen |
| Front | Ahp |
| Side | Yup |
| Back | Dwi (dwee) |
| Inward | Anuro (an-u-ro) |
| Inside | Ahn |

| | |
|---|---|
| Outward | Pakuro (pak-gu-ro) |
| Outside | Pakat |
| Upward | Wi (wee) |
| Downward | Naeryo (neh-rhee-o) |
| Opposite Edge | Yuk |
| Vertical | Sewo |
| Horizontal | Supyong |
| Hooking | Golcha |
| Rolling | Goolyo |
| Jumping | Dwi-myo |
| Fast techniques | Bal-ee kisool |
| Slow techniques | Chun-chun-nee kisool |
| Slow pushing | Tahn-jeon |
| Step in front | Yupuro omgyo (yup-u-ro) |
| Step behind | Bal-diro omgyo |
| Connecting | Eeh oh |
| Kneeling | Murrup gurro |
| Reverse (off the rear leg) | Bahndae |

## Terminology: Class Commands

| **English** | **Korean** |
|---|---|
| Attention | Charyot |
| Bow | Kyung-nyeh |
| Salute to the Flags | Kukiyeh daehaiyo kyung-nyeh, paro |
| Ready | Joon-bi |
| Stop | Keu-man |
| Begin | Shi-jak |
| Return (eyes front) | Paro |
| At ease, rest | She-yuh |
| Meditation | Bahn-sohn |
| Sit down | Ahn-jo |
| Stand up | Eero-su |
| About face | Dwee-ro dora |
| Change (switch) | Kyodae |

## Terminology: Counting

| | | | |
|---|---|---|---|
| **1** | Hana | **20** | Soomul |
| **2** | Dool | **30** | Solhum |
| **3** | Set | **40** | Mahun |
| **4** | Net | **50** | Swin |
| **5** | Tasot | **60** | Yesun |
| **6** | Yosot | **70** | Ilhun |

| | | | |
|---|---|---|---|
| **7** | Ilgope | **80** | Yodun |
| **8** | Yadul | **90** | Ahun |
| **9** | Ahope | **100** | Il-baek |
| **10** | Yol | | |

## Terminology: Greetings and Formalities

| **English** | **Korean** |
|---|---|
| Thank you | Kam-sa-ham-ni da |
| You're welcome | Chon-man-e-yo |
| Hello | An-nyong-ha-se-yo (Ahn youngha say yoh) |
| Goodbye (leaving) | An-nyong-hi Ka-se-yo (Ahn young ee Kah sayyoh) |
| Goodbye (staying) | An-nyong-hi Gye-se-yo (Ahn young ee Gay say yoh) |
| Congratulations | Chook-ha-ham-ni da |

## Terminology: Categories of Techniques

| **English** | **Korean** |
|---|---|
| Technique | Kisool (key-sool) |
| Stance | Sogi |
| Block | Makgi |
| Strike | Chirugi (thrusting strike) or Darigi (slashing strike) |
| Kick | Chagi |
| Throw | Mechiki |
| Fall | Nakbop |
| Lock | Cho-igi |
| Pull | Dan gigi |
| Grab | Chopki |
| Release | Pulgi |
| Trap | Olgami |

## Terminology: Stances

| **English** | **Korean** |
|---|---|
| Stance | Sogi |
| Open stance | Palcha sogi (feet turned outward)<br>Ahn palcha sogi (feet turned inward slightly) |
| Closed stance | Moa sogi (feet together) |
| Vertical stance | Soo jik sogi (feet close together but not touching) |
| Parallel stance | Narani sogi |
| One-legged stance | Hak dari sogi (leg up in chamber position)<br>Han bal sogi (leg in the air, any position) |

| | |
|---|---|
| Front stance | Ahp sogi |
| Horse stance | Kima sogi |
| Back stance | Dwi sogi (dui sogi) |
| Kneeling stance | Murrup gurro sogi |
| Cat stance | Goyangi sogi |
| X-stance | Kyocha sogi |
| Fixed stance | Kojung sogi |
| Closed ready stance | Moa joon-bi sogi |
| Open ready stance | Palcha joon-bi sogi |
| Fighting stance | Daeryon sogi |

## Terminology: Blocks

| **English** | **Korean** |
|---|---|
| Block | Makgi |
| Low section block | Hadan palmok makgi |
| Mid-section block | Chungdan palmok makgi |
| High section block | Sahngdan palmok makgi |
| Guarding block | Daebi makgi |
| Forearm block | Palmok makgi |
| Outside forearm block | Pakat palmok makgi |
| Inside forearm block | Ahn palmok makgi |
| Twin forearm block (box block) | Sahng sohn palmok makgi |
| Double forearm block (augmented) | Kodoro makgi |
| Wedging forearm block | Hecho palmok makgi |
| X-forearm block | Kyocha palmok makgi |
| W-shape block | San makgi |
| Circular scooping block | Tollyo turo (doo-ro) makgi |
| Pressing block | Noolyo Makgi |
| Knifehand block | Sohn-kal makgi |
| Double knifehand block | Dool sohn-kal makgi |
| Twin knifehand block (box block) | Sahng sohn sohn-kal makgi |
| Wedging (spreading) knifehand block | Hecho sohn-kal makgi |
| X-knifehand block | Kyocha sohn-kal makgi |
| Reverse knifehand (ridgehand) block | Yuk sohn-kal makgi |
| Hooking block | Golcha makgi |
| Palm heel block | Sohn-bahdok makgi |
| Palm heel pressing block | Sohn-bahdok noolyo makgi |
| Palm heel pushing block | Sohn-bahdok miro makgi |
| Palm heel scooping block | Sohn-bahdok turo (doo-ro) makgi |
| U-shape block (pole or staff block) | Mongdungi makgi |
| U-shape grasp (pole or staff grab) | Mongdungi chopgi |
| Waist block | Hori makgi |
| Face block | Olgool makgi |

| | |
|---|---|
| Arc hand block | Bandal sohn makgi |
| Double arc hand block | Dool bandal sohn makgi |
| Rising (upward) arc hand block | Wi bandal sohn makgi |
| 9-shape block | Kutcha makgi |
| Deflection block | Bahn sah chakyong makgi |
| Corkscrew trap | Kama toe olgami |

## Terminology: Strikes

| **English** | **Korean** |
|---|---|
| Any straight or linear technique | Chirugi (chi-ru-gi) |
| Any arcing or hooking strike | Darigi (deh-rigi) |
| | |
| Front punch | Ahp joomok chirugi |
| Reverse forefist punch | Bahndae ahp joomok chirugi |
| Side punch | Yup joomok chirugi |
| Vertical punch | Sewo joomok chirugi |
| Twin vertical punch | Sahng sohn sewo joomok chirugi |
| Vertical backfist strike | Sewo deung joomok darigi |
| Downward backfist strike | Naeryo deung joomok darigi |
| Spin backfist strike | Dwi tollyo deung joomok darigi |
| Uppercut strike | Twijibo (di ji bo) darigi |
| Turning punch | Tollyo ahp joomok darigi |
| Four knuckle fist strike | Pyung joomok chirugi |
| Hammerfist strike | Meh joomok darigi |
| Fore knuckle punch (1st knuckle) | Inji joomok chirugi |
| Twin uppercut strike | Sahng sohn joomok twijibo (di ji bo) darigi |
| Middle knuckle strike | Bam joomok chirugi |
| | |
| Knifehand strike | Sohn-kal darigi |
| Vertical knifehand strike | Sewo sohn-kal darigi |
| Spinning knifehand strike | Dwi tollyo sahn-kal darigi |
| Open backhand strike | Dwi sohn deung darigi |
| Thumb strike | Om ji sohn-garak darigi |
| Palm heel strike | Sohn-bahdak chirugi |
| Arc hand strike | Bandal sohn chirugi |
| | |
| Spearhand strike | Sohn-gut chirugi |
| Spearhand uppercut strike | Sohn-gut twijibo darigi |
| Twin spearhand uppercut strike | Sahng sohn-gut twijibo darigi |
| Vertical spearhand strike | Sewo sohn-gut chirugi |
| Single spearfinger strike | Sohn garak hana chirugi |
| Double spearfinger strike | Sohn garak dool chirugi |
| Ridgehand strike | Yuk sohn-kal darigi |
| Ridgehand strike—inward | Anuro yuk sohn-kal darigi |

| | |
|---|---|
| Ridgehand strike—outward | Pakuro uk sohn-kal darigi |
| Elbow strike | Palkumchi darigi |
| Front elbow strike | Ahp palkumchi darigi |
| Side elbow strike | Yup palkumchi darigi |
| Back elbow strike (toward rear) | Dwi palkumchi darigi |
| Rising elbow strike (upward) | Wi palkumchi darigi |
| Downward elbow strike | Naeryo palkumchi darigi |
| | |
| U-shape punch (attack) | De gutcha chirugi |
| Neck grab | Mok chopgi |
| Head grab | Kol chopgi |
| Outside forearm strike | Pakat palmok chirugi |

## Terminology: Kicks

| **English** | **Korean** |
|---|---|
| Kick | Chagi |
| Stretching kick | Chaolliki |
| | |
| Front stretch kick | Ahp chaolliki |
| Side stretch kick | Yup choalliki |
| Back stretch kick | Dwi chaolliki |
| | |
| Front kick | Ahp chagi |
| Double front kick | Dool ahp chagi |
| | |
| Crescent kick (inside to outside) | Ahp yuk tollyo chagi |
| Crescent kick (outside to inside) | Ahp tollyo chagi |
| Spinning crescent kick (inside to outside) | Dwi tollyo ahp yuk tollyo chagi |
| Rear leg crescent kick (outside to inside) | Dwi bal ahp tollyo chagi |
| Rear leg crescent kick (inside to outside) | Dwi bal ahp yuk tollyo chagi |
| | |
| Side kick | Yup chagi |
| Step behind side kick | Bal-diro omgyo yup chagi |
| Connecting side kick | Eeh oh yup chagi |
| Side kick ready position | Yup chagi joon-bi |
| Double side kick | Dool yup chagi |
| Rear leg side kick | Dwi bal yup chagi |
| Spin side kick | Dwi tollyo yup chagi |
| Pushing side kick | Miro yup chagi |
| Kneeling side kick | Murrup gurro yup chagi |
| | |
| Roundhouse kick | Tollyo hagi |
| Step in front roundhouse kick | Yupuro omgyo tollyo chagi |
| Rear leg roundhouse kick | De bal tollyo chagi |

| | |
|---|---|
| Back kick | Dwi chagi |
| Kneeling back kick | Murrup gurro dwi chagi |
| Hook kick | Golcha chagi |
| Spinning hook kick | Dwi tollyo golcha chagi |
| Spinning heel kick (back wheel kick) | Dwi tollyo chagi |
| Kneeling spinning heel kick (spin reap) | Murrup gurro dwi tollyo chagi |
| Kneeling spinning hook kick | Murrup gurro dwi tollyo golcha chagi |
| Twisting kick | Pi-turyo chagi |
| Axe kick | Ji go chagi |
| Pressing kick | Noolyo chagi |
| Consecutive kick | Yonsok chagi |
| Stomping kick | Pahlba chagi |
| Jumping side kick | Dwi-myo yup chagi |
| Jumping front kick | Dwi-myo ahp chagi |
| Jumping roundhouse kick | Dwi-myo tollyo chagi |
| Double jumping kicks | Dool dwi-myo … (ahp, yup, dwi, etc.) |
| Jump hook kick | Dwi-myo golcha chagi |
| Jump spinning back kick | Dwi-myo dwi tollyo chagi |
| Jump spinning hook kick | Dwi-myo dwi tollyo golcha chagi |
| Jump spin crescent kick | Dwi-myo dwi tollyo ahp yuk tollyo chagi |
| Tornado kick | Toneido chagi |

## Terminology: Falling

Note: Japanese terminology is commonly used for throwing and falling techniques; please see Appendix B.

| **English** | **Korean** |
|---|---|
| Fall | Nakbop |
| Backward falling | Hoobang nakbop |
| Forward falling | Jeonbang nakbop |
| Side falling | Cheukbang nakbop |
| Forward roll falling | Jeonbang hejeon nakbop |

# Appendix B: Japanese Terminology

Because Kyuki-Do draws from the Japanese arts of Judo and Jiu Jitsu, Japanese terminology for throwing and falling techniques is commonly utilized. The following is a list of Japanese terminology.

## Japanese Terminology: General

| English | Japanese |
|---|---|
| Gentle Way | Judo |
| Maximum efficiency/minimum effort | Seirokyu Zenyu |
| Mutual welfare and benefit Or "you and I shining together" | Jita Kyoei |
| Gentle System | Jiu Jitsu |
| Training hall | Dojo |
| Offensive partner | Tori |
| Defensive partner | Uke |
| Instructor | Sensei |
| Belt | Obi |
| Uniform | Gi |
| Free exercise | Randori |
| Energy yell | Kiai |
| Off balance | Kuzushi |
| Step-ins | Uchikomi |
| School | Ryu |
| Grade | Kyu |
| Degree | Dan |
| Judo student | Judoka |

## Japanese Terminology: Tournaments and Class Commands

| English | Japanese |
|---|---|
| Judo contest | Shiai |
| Start or begin | Hajime |
| Stop | Matte |
| Attention | Kyotsuke |
| Bow | Rei |
| Call for decision | Hantei |
| Pin has been applied | Osaekomi |
| Pin has been broken | Osaekomi Tocada |

## Japanese Terminology: Categories of Techniques

| English | Japanese |
|---|---|

| | |
|---|---|
| Technique | Waza |
| Throwing technique | Nage waza |
| Standing technique | Tachi waza |
| Hip technique | Koshi waza |
| Hand technique | Te waza |
| Foot technique | Ashi waza |
| Sacrifice technique | Sutemi waza |
| Back sacrifice technique | Ma sutemi waza |
| Side sacrifice technique | Yoko sutemi waza |
| Grappling technique | Katame waza |
| Pinning technique | Osae komi waza |
| Strangling technique | Jime waza |
| Joint locking technique | Kansetsu waza |
| Falling technique | Ukemi waza |

## Japanese Terminology: Throws

| English | Japanese |
|---|---|
| **Hip techniques** | **Koshi waza** |
| Floating hip | Uki goshi |
| Sweeping hip | Harai goshi |
| Lifting pulling hip | Tsurikomi goshi |
| Sleeve lifting pulling hip | Sode tsurikomi goshi |
| Springing hip | Hane goshi |
| Major hip | O goshi |
| Back hip | Ushiro goshi |
| Hip shift | Utsuri goshi |
| Lifting hip | Tsuri goshi |
| High lift | Dakiage |
| Hip wheel | Koshi guruma |
| **Hand techniques** | **Te waza** |
| Body drop | Tai otoshi |
| One armed shoulder throw | Ippon seoi nage |
| Two handed shoulder throw | Morote seoi nage |
| Shoulder wheel | Kata guruma |
| Floating drop | Uki otoshi |
| Corner drop | Sumi otoshi |
| Scooping throw | Suke nage |
| Belt drop | Obi otoshi |
| Shoulder drop | Seoi otoshi |
| Mountain storm | Yama arashi |
| Two handed reap | Morote gari |
| One hand drop | Kuchiki taoshi |

| | |
|---|---|
| Heel reversal | Kibisu gaeshi |
| Inner thigh slip | Uchi mata sukashi |
| Minor inner reversal | Ko uchi gaeshi |
| | |
| **Foot techniques** | **Ashi waza** |
| Knee wheel | Hiza guruma |
| Major inner reap | O uchi gari |
| Major outer reap | O soto gari |
| Propping lifting pulling ankle | Sasae tsurikomi ashi |
| Sliding foot sweep | Okuri ashi harai |
| Advancing foot sweep | De ashi harai |
| Minor inner reap | Ko uchi gari |
| Minor outer reap | Ko soto gare |
| Minor outer hook | Ko soto gake |
| Knee wheel | Ashi guruma |
| Inner thigh | Uchi mata |
| Sweeping lifting pulling ankle | Harai tsurikomi ashi |
| Major wheel | O guruma |
| Major outer wheel | O soto guruma |
| Major outer drop | O soto otoshi |
| Darting swallow reversal | Tsubame gaeshi |
| Major outer reversal | O soto gaeshi |
| Major inner reversal | O uchi gaeshi |
| Springing hip reversal | Hane goshi gaeshi |
| Sweeping hip reversal | Harai goshi gaeshi |
| Inner thigh reversal | Uchi mata gaeshi |
| | |
| **Back sacrifice techniques** | **Ma sutemi waza** |
| Circle throw | Tomoe nage |
| Back throw | Ura nage |
| Corner reversal | Sumi gaeshi |
| Draw pull reversal | Hikkomi gaeshi |
| Rice bale reversal | Tawara gaeshi |
| | |
| **Side sacrifice techniques** | **Yoko sutemi waza** |
| Floating technique | Uki waza |
| Side hook | Yoko gake |
| Side wheel | Yoko guruma |
| Valley drop | Tani otoshi |
| Side separation | Yoko wakare |
| Side drop | Yoko otoshi |
| Springing wraparound | Hane makikomi |
| High lift separation | Daki wakare |
| Flying scissors | Kani basami |
| Outer wraparound | Soto makikomi |
| Major outer wraparound | O soto makikomi |

| | |
|---|---|
| Inner wraparound | Uchi makikomi |
| Inner thigh wraparound | Uchi mata makikomi |
| One leg entanglement | Kawazu gake |
| Sweeping wraparound | Harai makikomi |

## Japanese Terminology: Grappling Techniques

| English | Japanese |
|---|---|
| **Pinning techniques** | **Osae komi waza** |
| Scarf hold | Kesa gatame |
| Pillow scarf hold | Makura kesa gatame |
| Modified shoulder hold | Kuzuri kata gatame |
| Chest hold | Mune gatame |
| Knee on stomach hold | Hiza hara gatame |
| Modified chest hold | Kuzuri mune gatame |
| Modified side four corner hold | Kuzuri yoko shiho gatame |
| Upper four corner hold | Kami shiho gatame |
| Modified upper four corner hold | Kuzuri kami shiho gatame |
| Reverse scarf hold | Ushiro kesa gatame |
| Vertical four corner hold | Tate shiho gatame |
| Shoulder hold | Kata gatame |
| Side four corner hold | Yoko shiho gatame |
| | |
| **Strangling techniques** | **Shime waza** |
| Normal cross choke | Nami juji jime |
| Half cross choke | Kata juji jime |
| Reverse cross choke | Gyaku juji jimc |
| Naked strangle | Hadaka jime |
| Sliding lapel strangle | Okuri eri jime |
| Singlc wing choke | Kata ha jime |
| One hand choke | Katate jime |
| Two hand choke | Ryote jime |
| Sleeve wheel choke | Sode garuma jime |
| Thrusting choke | Tsukkomi jime |
| Triangle choke | Sankaku jime |
| Body choke | Do jime |
| | |
| **Joint locking techniques** | **Kansetsu waza** |
| Entangled armlock | Ude garami |
| Cross armlock | Ude hishigi juji gatame |
| Arm armlock | Ude hishigi ude gatame |
| Knee armlock | Ude hishigi hiza gatame |
| Armpit armlock | Ude hishigi waki gatame |
| Stomach armlock | Ude hishigi hara gatame |
| Foot armlock | Ude hishigi ashi gatame |
| Hand armlock | Ude hishigi te gatame |

| | |
|---|---|
| Triangle armlock | Ude hishigi sankaku gatame |
| Entangled leglock | Ude garami |

## Japanese Terminology: Falls

| **English** | **Japanese** |
|---|---|
| **Falling techniques** | **Ukemi waza** |
| Back fall | Koho ukemi |
| Side fall | Sokuho ukemi |
| Front fall | Zenpo ukemi |
| Front roll | Zenpo kaiten |

# Appendix C: Grand Master Kim's Personal Philosophy

In this section, Grand Master Kim would like to share a portion of his personal philosophy, which is based on traditional Korean religion. Grand Master Kim stresses that this is only the philosophy that he has developed based on his own goals and on the experiences that he has had. Because there are so many variables in our lives, it is very unlikely that other people will have the same philosophy. He also wishes to note that Kyuki-Do students and members of the Federation do **not** need to adopt this belief system; it is being provided solely so that the student of Kyuki-Do may gain a greater understanding into the culture, tradition and mindset that has gone into the creation of the art.

Grand Master Kim also believes that when people are able to express and share their views in an open manner, they are better able to understand and appreciate one another. It is in that spirit that Grand Master Kim offers us a glimpse of the philosophy that provides the framework for his life, so that the students of Kyuki-Do might better understand him.

## Elements, Energy and Environment

There are five elements that are reflected in the world around us. These elements include Fire, Water, Wood, Metal and Earth, and they make up the universe.

Each element has a corresponding energy or environment associated with it: energy of Wind (Wood), energy of Heat (Fire), energy of Cool (Water), energy of Moist (Earth) and energy of Dry (Metal). These energies and elements can be found in every thing in the universe, both animate and inanimate, and the traits that they embody can be found in every action or event that occurs.

The five elements and energies form the building blocks of everything that exists, both physically and spiritually. The interaction of these elements defines the world we live in.

## Eum and Yang, and the Balance

Eum and Yang symbolize an unending balance between opposites: between heaven and earth, male and female, positive and negative, night and day. All things have elements of both Eum and Yang within them; even within Eum there is Yang, and even within Yang there is Eum. This is symbolized in the Chinese version of the symbol, which includes a black circle within the white teardrop and a white circle within the black teardrop. This means that in even the worst of people there is some amount of good; it is the responsibility of the instructor to find what is good in a student and cultivate that goodness to help the student grow and mature.

The idea of balance is of great importance. All things have a natural state of balance or equilibrium, and we must seek out that state of balance. Only when the energies within us are in balance are we able to awaken and fulfill our purpose.

## Divine Principle

There is an underlying principle or order to the universe. All living things have their own purposes, but these purposes work together in accordance with the Divine Principle.

The interactions between the energies of the world and the Divine Principle are what make human beings what they are. It is what gives us our thoughts and emotions. In turn, these thoughts and emotions can then influence how the energies affect us, leading to an unending cycle.

For human beings, the Divine Principle dictates that our purpose is to be awake and enlightened, and to harness the natural energies of the universe to turn the negative into the positive. This ability to use and change the natural energy of the world is unique to humans. It is this that allows us to grow, to create and to make the world a better place, and to awaken others to their potential to grow and improve. This is our purpose.

## *Appendix D: The Meaning and History of the AKF Black Belt Certificate*

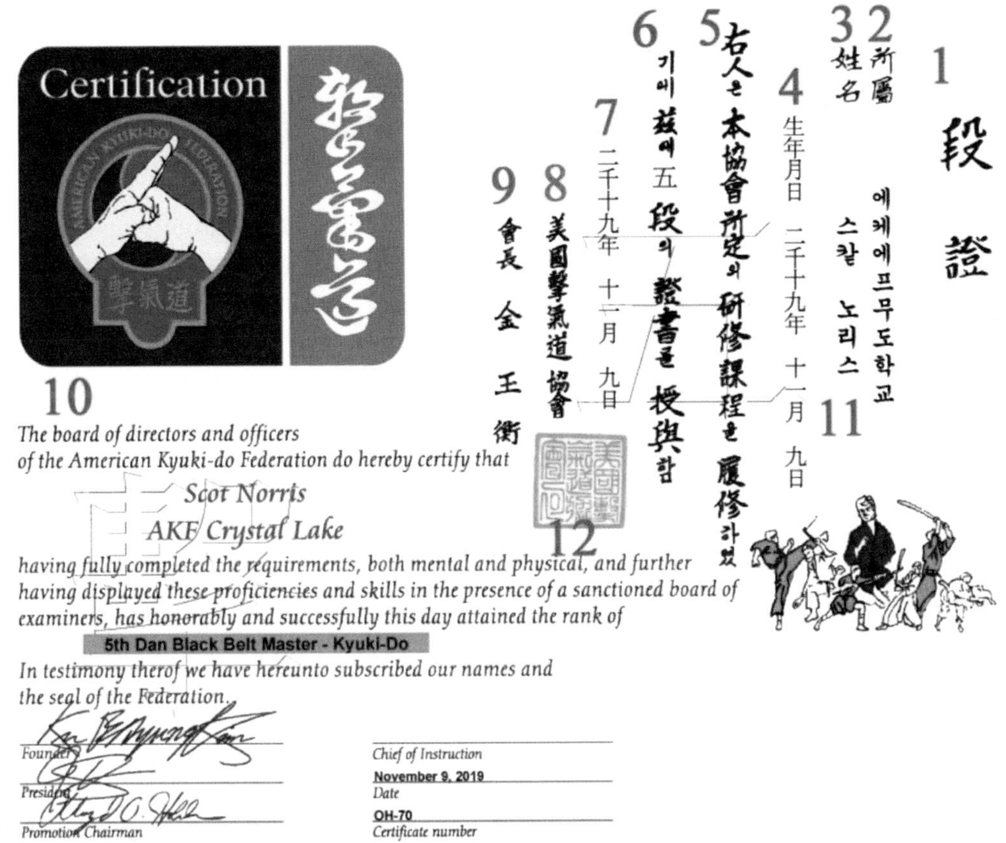
Certification

擊氣道

段 證

所屬 에케에프무도학교

姓名 스캇 노리스

生年月日 二千十九年 十一月 九日

右人은 本協會所定의 硏修課程을 履修하였

기에 五段의 證書를 授與함

二千十九年 十一月 九日

美國擊氣道 協會

會長 金王衛

*The board of directors and officers of the American Kyuki-do Federation do hereby certify that*

*Scot Norris*

*AKF Crystal Lake*

*having fully completed the requirements, both mental and physical, and further having displayed these proficiencies and skills in the presence of a sanctioned board of examiners, has honorably and successfully this day attained the rank of*

**5th Dan Black Belt Master - Kyuki-Do**

*In testimony therof we have hereunto subscribed our names and the seal of the Federation.*

Founder | Chief of Instruction

President | November 9, 2019 Date

Promotion Chairman | OH-70 Certificate number

| **Column** | **Meaning** |
|---|---|
| 1. | Black Belt Certification (Chinese) |
| 2. | Academy (Chinese) then Your Academy Name (in Korean) |
| 3. | Name (Chinese) then Your Actual Name (in Korean) |
| 4. | Date of Birth (Chinese) |
| 5/6. | "…having fully completed the requirements…has honorably and successfully this day attained the rank of 5th Dan Master Kyuki-Do" (in Chinese and Korean) |
| 7. | Promotion Date (Chinese) |
| 8. | American Kyuki-Do Federation (Chinese) |
| 9. | President Emeritus Ok Hyung Kim (Chinese) |
| 10. | The faint outlined symbol behind the English text represents the art that you have earned rank in. For some arts this is written in Korean and for others it is in Chinese. |
| 11. | At rank of 5th Dan Master and above, an additional faint outlined symbol is added behind the Asian characters, representing the rank number. |
| 12. | American Kyuki-Do Federation Stamp of Approval |

Grand Master Ken Ok Hyung Kim first produced the AKF Black Belt certificates in 1979 by hand. After years of producing the certificates by hand, Grand Master Kim, with the help of

Master Kwang Soo Kim and Master Han Suk Lee, started using a drafting letter tracer and India ink to produce the AKF certificates more efficiently and consistently. In the early 1990s, Master John Cantin assisted Grand Master Kim with modernizing the production of the certificates by printing the certificates via computer.

For historical reasons, Chinese and Korean characters appear in the AKF certificate. In the 15th century, Sejong the Great, the fourth king of the Joseon Dynasty, commissioned the creation of Korea's own alphabet, known as Hangul. Prior to the use of Hangul, Koreans had used Chinese characters (known as "Hanja" in Korean, or "Kanji" in Japanese) and native phonetic systems for their written language. As the majority of Korea's historical documents and literature are written in Hanja, it was necessary to study Hanja in order to be literate in Korean. It wasn't until the 20th century that Hangul replaced Hanja as the official Korean written language. This is the reason why Chinese and Korean are represented in the AKF certificate.

Made in the USA
Monee, IL
05 November 2021